The Devil's Details

The Devil's Details

A *History* of *Footnotes*

Chuck Zerby

INVISIBLE CITIES PRESS
Montpelier, Vermont

Invisible Cities Press
50 State Street
Montpelier, Vermont 05602
www.invisiblecitiespress.com

Library of Congress Cataloging-in-Publication Data

Zerby, Chuck.
The devil's details : a history of footnotes / Chuck Zerby.
p. cm.
Includes bibliographical references (p.   )
ISBN 1-931229-05-8 (cloth : alk. paper)
Bibliographical citations—History. I. Title.

PN171.F56 Z47 2001
907'.2—dc21   2001039401

Some material in "The Endangered Footonote" was first published
as an editorial in the *New York Times*. Reprinted with permission.

MANUFACTURED IN THE UNITED STATES OF AMERICA

Book design by Tim Jones
for Sterling Hill Productions

FIRST EDITION

In memory of Angela Carmela Mascolo

Contents

Acknowledgments

JANE, MY WIFE, LOVE, and first reader, has been an indispensable companion during this adventure. My children, Karen and Christopher, deserve thanks for being who they are and for taking me out to dinner. Ann Brandon, as an editor at Invisible Press, was the first to see what one sketchy chapter could become, and coaxed and prodded a sometimes balky and sometimes confused writer into getting it done. My workshop readers supported and helped me when I most needed it, as always. Joe Bakanauskas did some valuable research on short notice and with vague instructions. All of the people at Invisible Cities Press were enthusiastic, helpful, and patient. And finally I want to thank Matt Zimet, whose wit and precise eye inform this project.

1

The Endangered Footnote

THE NEED FOR AN ADEQUATE* book on footnotes is
obvious. One of the earliest and most ingenious inventions of humankind, the footnote has been for centuries
an indispensable tool of the scholar and a source of endlessly
varied delight for the layperson. The lack until now of a substantial and appropriately annotated study of its nature, its
history, its friends and enemies can only be ascribed to complacency. Annotators and literary connoisseurs simply have
assumed too easily the continuing survival of this important
adjunct to the printing press.

Such complacency is no longer possible. Gone is the time
when the Reverend John Hodgson, the distinguished nineteenth-century historian, could unselfconsciously devote one
quarto of his multivolume account of Northumberland
County (England) to a single gigantic footnote on the Roman
Wall.[1] Nor could the equally well-known historian Edward

---

* An adequate history will be a humanistic history: one that does not
restrict the footnote to the bare-bones function of referring the reader
to cited material. Such a restricted view of the footnote is as inadequate
as would be the notion that an X ray of the human body reveals the full
import of the human being.

1. See M. H. Dodds, "Footnotes," *Notes and Queries*, 19 October 1910. I
have not located the actual footnote volume of the Reverend Hodgson.

Gibbon expect any longer to be congratulated for allocating one-fourth of his space in *The Decline and Fall of the Roman Empire* to footnotes. Footnotes distress publishers, who unfortunately lurk behind every book. They find notes unsightly, costly, forbidding. Toward the end of the twentieth century, publishers foisted upon the reader a recondite game to further discourage the use of notes. The game goes like this: First you must fix in your mind the number of the footnote, say 27, then you have to remember the page number on which footnote 27 appears, say page 85. Then you must turn to the back of the book, trying to keep your place with an inserted finger, and scan page after page until you discover one headed "Footnotes for Pages 81–107." By this time you have forgotten the footnote number so you must scramble back to the original page and seek it out again, sitting small and sulkily, in the text. Only enthusiasts of acrostic puzzles and nine-digit ZIP codes can possibly persist in this game.

So complicated have publishers made the arrangement of notes, in fact, that help from sophisticated mathematics has been required. Utilizing the theory of sets and subsets, a so-called Hoffman system has been devised to guide annotators in the placement of their notes. It provides an intricate flow chart complete with little boxes and directional arrows—the kind of thing General Motors uses to keep track of its spare parts.*

---

* There is no need for flow charts if the convenience of the reader is kept firmly in mind. The present writer has used reference marks to indicate explanatory notes; he has used numerals to indicate notes that are wholly or in large part references. Thus these later can be easily skipped should the reader be uninterested in checking the author's scholarship. Also for the convenience of the reader, *ibid.* is used but not *op. cit.* or *loc. cit.* A cluster of *ibid*s is decorative and alerts the reader to a cluster of references to the same title. However, *op. cit.* and *loc. cit.* often entail a frus-

Several firms have gone so far as to announce that they will not burden their texts with footnotes, as if conferring a favor upon their readers. Others have slyly encouraged a writer or two to put up a Web site for the footnotes that have been refused the hospitality of the book itself. The notion seems to be that this way the scholar can find the "dull" citations if needed while the general reader can have an uninterrupted *good read.*

We know this to be nonsense, of course. The layperson as well as the scholar enjoys footnotes. They can be charming, an encouragement to read on, worth every penny of the extra expense.

The Letters of Evelyn Waugh might easily have been published without any interruption by its editor. But then we never would have learned that the "pornographer" whom Waugh said fed a horse vodka and got bitten for his pains was Norman Mailer. Nor would we have learned that Mailer—tracked down by the indefatigable editor—insisted that he had not been trying to get the horse drunk but was merely patting it.[2]

Such information keeps us reading, but the main job of the footnote is to interrupt. Simply interrupt.

A stern, no-nonsense lecture on the eighteenth-century belief that the universe was a smooth-running machine is being delivered. Suddenly, from the bottom of the page, a voice whispers, "It should be pointed out, however, that de la Mettrie, the author of the famous book *Man The Machine,* died of over eating and gout; he stoked the machine too

---

trating retreat back through pages already read in order to find the necessary reference.

2. Mark Amory, ed., *The Letters of Evelyn Waugh* (New Haven, Conn.: Ticknor & Fields, 1980), p. 573.

well."[3] The reader is intensely grateful for this human interruption.

Being human, authors sometimes miscalculate, of course, which is part of the charm of footnotes. That gentlest of philosophers, William James, once interrupted his discussion of the brain to reassure the reader. "Nothing is easier than to familiarize oneself with the mammalian brain," he said. "Get a Sheep's head, a small saw, chisel, and forceps . . . and unravel its parts."[4] Only a reader with a strong stomach will gain the assurance James intended.

Ironically, should the conspiracy to ease footnotes into extinction succeed, publishers' own interests will suffer. The absence of footnotes will discourage rather than attract the general reader, particularly when the text is difficult—the time when an interruption is most welcome.

In a fit of self-mortification, a friend of mine was trying to fight his way through an explanation of Kant's categorical imperative. The explanation, by an Oxford professor, was brief and kindly but after sixty pages my friend's eyes glazed over. Fortunately, a footnote interrupted. "It is extraordinary," the professor said, "how early the human mind seems able to grasp the universality of moral law. A small boy of five, not especially conspicuous either for goodness or intelligence, was presented on a flag day with several flags. One of these he was kind enough to give me. Later he gave another to his sister, who rewarded him with a sixpence. Whereupon—surely on the assumption that his sister's action was a manifestation of universal law (even if

---

3. Daniel Bell, *The Coming of Post-Industrial Society: A Venture in Social Forecasting* (New York: Basic Books, 1973), p. 349.

4. William James, *The Principles of Psychology* (Chicago: Encyclopedia Britannica, 1952), p. 7.

this was not without advantages to himself)—he asserted, 'If G. gives me a sixpence, the Professor will have to give me a sixpence, too.'"[5] My friend felt as if a window had suddenly been opened in a rather stuffy room; children's voices, distant band music drifted in. Refreshed, he managed to start marching through the text again—someday he may even finish it.

Amusement, charm, a chance to rest: These gifts alone should make us grateful for the footnote. But the footnote is also educational. If it opens windows to bands and parades, it also lets us peer into the inner workshops of scholars. A few glimpses of what goes on there should convince anyone that it is an entirely human activity, that the impersonal recitation of ideas or seamless narrative a text sometimes allows us to enjoy is an illusion—as much of an illusion as a Fred Astaire dance across tables and chairs, up walls, and across ceilings. Footnotes let us hear the missteps of biases, and hear pathos, subtle decisions, scandal and anger.

This function of the footnote is important enough to require a few immediate illustrations, though many more will be sprinkled throughout this book.*

Bias: In 1838 Edmund Lodge, Esq., K.H., Norroy King of Arms, F.S.A., compiled for our benefit a book of documents illustrating "British history, biography, and manners in the reigns of Henry VIII, Edward VI, Mary, Elizabeth, & James I." They were "selected from the mss. of the noble families of

---

5. H. J. Paton, *The Categorical Imperative: A Study in Kant's Moral Philosophy* (New York: Harper & Row, 1967), p. 69.

* That the footnote is not just an artifact of scholarship nor its survival the concern of the scholar is a major theme of this book. Humanism and the layperson have as much at stake as scholars in the struggle to keep the footnote alive.

Howard, Talbot, and Cecil."[6] Only the unsophisticated would enter the book without recognizing that the selections may have been skewed by the taste and temperament of its distinguished Victorian editor. But by the time we arrive at page 316, we may forget that, like a reporter who travels for a season with the same baseball team, say the Red Sox, Edmund Lodge, Esq., may cease to be a recorder of the team's hits and pitches and become a fan. ("Joe DiMaggio may have hit in 56 straight games," such a writer might argue, "but he didn't join up after Pearl Harbor; Roger Maris may have hit 61 home runs but he didn't fight in the Korean War; Ted Williams hit over .400 for a season *and* served his country twice." This kind of writing is even-handedness to a Boston reporter.)

Fortunately, on page 316, a footnote returns us to our skepticism. A report from the earl of Shrewsbury to the Privy Council states: "If money could have been had in these parts, I would assuredly for the present need have mortgaged or sold any land or things I have. . . ."[7] At the bottom of the page Edmund Lodge, Esq., tosses his hat and cheers. "The reader will not hesitate to join with me here in a just tribute of veneration to the departed spirit of true patriotism."[8] Well, yes, unless the reader is a Yankee fan.

---

6. Edmund Lodge, Esq., K.H., Norroy King of Arms, F.S.A., *Illustrations of British History, Biography, and Manners, in the Reigns of Henry VIII, Edward VI, Mary, Elizabeth, & James I, exhibited in a series of Original Papers, selected from the Mss., of the Noble Families of Howard, Talbot, and Cecil; containing among a variety of interesting pieces, a great part of the correspondence of Elizabeth and Her Ministers with George Sixth Earl of Shrewsbury, during the fifteen years in which Mary Queen of Scots, remained in his custody* (London: John Chidley, 1837), p. 316.

7. Ibid.

8. Ibid.

Pedanticism: Hegel, author of *Encyklopadie der Philosphischen im Grundrisse (Encyclopedia of the Philosophical Sciences in Outline)* and the late headmaster of a boarding school in Nuremberg, Germany, was a connoisseur of abstractions; in fact, some of his readers have come to believe that for Hegel only the mind was real. In a discussion of the beauty of nature, Hegel may have given support to that belief. He first suggests that "we call animal organisms bizarre, if the way their organs are connected falls outside what we have already often seen previously. . . ." Then he offers, as an example, "a fish whose disproportionately large body ends in a short tail and whose eyes are together on one side of the head." The fish might have seemed simply a figment of Hegel's real or unreal mind had not his translator consulted an English colleague—perhaps a fish-and-chips devotee—who pointed out that "the description of the fish fits a Dover sole."[9] This footnote both indicates the need for dogged and careful scholarship and recognizes the danger of pedanticism; readers who think scholars have an easy life are immediately put on notice. Scholars, like trapeze artists, risk humiliation—if not something worse.

Scandal: We might believe that Daniel Bell, famous for *The Coming of Post-Industrial Society* and other pronouncements, is simply a Harvard professor who sits quietly in his office explaining our past and forecasting our future. Certainly the number of words making their way out of his office and into print suggests a deskbound existence.

Bell's life, however, has not been entirely sedentary. In 1959 he was in Salzburg, Austria, dangerously close to the Iron Curtain. There, injudiciously, he let be seen a preliminary

---

9. G. W. F. Hegel, *Aesthetics: Lectures on Fine Art*, trans. T. M. Knox (Oxford: Clarendon Press, 1975), p. 12.

blueprint of the future postindustrial society. Unauthorized eyes were watching. On his return to the café society of Cambridge, Massachusetts, as he ruefully admits in a footnote, his plans "inexplicably . . . turned up as a citation in the volume published by the Czechoslovak Academy of Science on the scientific and technological revolutions which were creating a post-industrial society."[10] One suspects disingenuousness on Bell's part: The ubiquitousness of industrial espionage is sufficiently known that his experience is far from inexplicable.

Clash of egos: A scholar's life is not for the timid. A somewhat sad illustration of this occurred many years ago. Historians were engaged in a furious conflict set off by a recently unearthed confidential memo submitted to the U.S. Intelligence Bureau during World War I by John Dewey, the philosopher and Vermonter. (The intricacies of the dispute are no more necessary for the general reader to grasp than a knowledge of how to load a musket is required by *War and Peace*.) A short volley of criticism, supported by fifty rapidly fired footnotes, was directed at one of the combatants by an inexperienced graduate student. The response was a barrage of eighty-four notes, at least one of which struck home. "Zerby," the assaulted scholar's note exploded, "misquotes me, accidentally, I suspect by substituting 'which' for 'that'."[11] The wound inflicted should not be minimized. Grammar— despite the considerable evidence to the contrary—remains

---

10. Daniel Bell, *The Coming of Post-Industrial Society: A Venture in Social Forecasting* (New York: Basic Books, 1973), p. 36.

11. Clarence J. Karier, "John Dewey and the New Liberalism: Some Reflections and Responses," *History of Education Quarterly,* winter 1957, p. 442. See also Charles L. Zerby, "John Dewey and the Polish Question: A Response to the Revisionist Historians," *History of Education Quarterly,* pp. 17–30.

important to graduate students. The imputation that the error was an accident instead of a subtle tactical move seems to have been devastating: "that" graduate student's name never appeared again in a scholarly journal.

The list of how the footnote humanizes scholarship could be extended nearly indefinitely. Indeed, for those of us who have followed its evolution with some care, the temptation is simply to extend the list *ad infinitum*.

We must recognize, however, that footnotes can be mistrusted precisely because they reveal the inner workings of scholarship. This has been talked about quite openly by Thomas McFarland, a deft biographer and scholar of the Romantic period. In a nice little confessional of his, "Who Was Benjamin Whichcote? or, The Myth of Annotation," he recounts his own ambiguous relationship with the footnote. For one of his early books, he produced a manuscript of some eleven hundred typed pages, which we can surmise included about five hundred footnotes; subsequently he added another five hundred. "The Clarendon Press at that time," McFarland assures us, "was noted for the elegance of its printing and design. . . ."[12] This commitment to elegance led the publisher to suggest that some of the notes be jettisoned; the conscientious scholar refused. Next came a suggestion that some notes be combined and placed at the rear of the book. McFarland took this to heart—though perhaps in that heart of his pulsed the blood of Rube Goldberg, for as McFarland excised some notes he complicated the remaining. Some nineteen so-called excursus notes were added to the back of the book; these were essays "put together from cullings of reference and statements

---

12. Thomas McFarland, "Who Was Benjamin Whichcote? or, The Myth of Annotation," in *Annotation and Its Texts*, ed. Stephen A. Barney (Oxford, New York, and Toronto: Oxford University Press, 1991), p. 160.

on various topics." And after those were added endnotes that were not "cullings" but "individually dialogical essays."[13]

The experience, however, apparently disillusioned him. "The effect of the whole volume was somewhat parallel to the paradox of Achilles and the tortoise. No matter how assiduously one read, one never seemed to be able to reach the end of the book; it was particularly dispiriting for the type continually to become smaller as one tried to hasten forward. Indeed, I have sometimes wondered whether anyone except me and my editor has ever actually been able to read the book through."[14]

McFarland's charming self-doubts have had a profound influence on him. He more recently tried to persuade his publisher to put out a book of his without any notes at all— no footnotes, no endnotes, no excursus notes, just the plain, unadorned, continuous text. A brave move for a scholar, one akin to an actor appearing on stage alone, *sans* costume, *sans* makeup, *sans* props, just the actor, his script, and his audience. McFarland's courage is of less immediate interest to us, however, than the reasons he gives for his proud nakedness. His explanation takes us back to his school days when he, as he puts it with commendable meticulousness, "was unusually erratic or, not to put too firm a point on it, decidedly neurotic."[15] The academic label given him, he says (with what we imagine is a slight wince), was "brilliant but unsound."[16] Thus he piled up footnotes to defend his arguments "much as a soldier at the

---

13. Ibid., p. 161.
14. Ibid., p. 160.
15. Ibid., p. 163.
16. Ibid., p. 164.

front might throw up earthworks. . . ."[17] Earthworks: After years of labor any scholar[*] might delight in tossing away notes, much as a kid runs along the beach kicking down sand castles and squealing. What a sense of freedom they both must feel, the wind whipping their hair, squinty-eyed onlookers muttering.

But then in another place in his confession, McFarland changes himself from a free spirit running along the beach to a suspicious miser looking over his shoulder. "To be quite cynical," he quotes himself as having written his publisher at the time, "I really see no other need for footnotes than to allow scholarly readers to purloin my citations without having to give *me* a reference. Certainly the average interested reader . . . is pleased rather than put off by the absence of footnotes. It is only other scholars who cry for footnotes, for reasons that they would be hard put to defend."[18]

As tempting as it is to ascribe a hard-nosed, even commercial, motive to scholarly antagonism to footnotes, that is too easy. Anyone who has been around a practicing scholar knows there is more of the kid in his soul than the banker. (Many of them, for example, take summers off.) And always we should keep in mind that the footnote, like the haiku or terza rima, makes difficult and strict demands on the writer, however much pleasure it may give the reader. Impatience, even resentment, and certainly ambiguous feelings on the part of writers toward footnotes are to be expected.

---

17. Ibid.

* Particularly one, we should add, who before the days of the computer produced eleven hundred typed pages and a thousand notes to accompany them. Anyone who doubts the heroism of the precomputer scholar should try for a day inserting footnotes without the aid of his digital machine.

18. Ibid., p. 170.

McFarland expresses ambiguities not just in his autobiography but also in his metaphors and analogies; they are deeply set in his psyche indeed. Footnotes, on the one hand, are intended to be "an impregnable fortification";[19] on the other hand, they turn out not to be "steel cables woven into a gigantic interconnection of meaning" but in fact "connected to nothing."[20] They are "short and localized outriggers."[21] They come in and out of fashion as do bell-bottoms or stovepipes.[22] However, to try to ignore "footnote indicators" when reading can be "something like driving over a road with innumerable potholes."[23] The feeling that footnotes are trouble (and bone-rattling trouble at that)—maybe more trouble than they are worth—is unmistakable.

Scholars are often viewed as park rangers of footnotes; the notes are on their preserve and in their charge. But scholars are not entirely to be trusted. A notable example is the pioneering historian of the footnote, Anthony Grafton. His *The Footnote: A Curious History* is solid scholarship, an entertaining read, and a sophisticated defense of the footnote as scholarly tool. Alerted by our experience with McFarland to the fact that hidden and ambiguous feelings may be expressed in metaphor as they are in dreams, we can "psyche out" Grafton.

He turns out to be a terribly conflicted supporter of the footnote; his mind says one thing, his dreams something else. Early on a peculiar "low rumble" is ascribed to the footnote and the "rumble" compared to the dentist's drill's "high

---

19. Ibid., p. 164.
20. Ibid., p. 177.
21. Ibid.
22. See ibid., p. 162.
23. Ibid., p. 156.

whine";[24] enthusiastic annotators then are compared to "dentists who have become inured to inflicting pain and shedding blood. . . ."[25] We leave the dentist's office only to hear that the "production of footnotes" resembles "the disposal of waste products."[26] Next comes a comparison of the footnote to a fish that few readers bother to trawl for, then to a shabby podium, a carafe of water, a "rambling, inaccurate introduction."[27] That each of these comparisons is in the service of a legitimate insight and that each extends our understanding of the footnote does not conceal the "low rumble" of hostility emanating from this scholar's prose.[*]

It is true that when Grafton's story reaches the eighteenth century, the seductiveness of that century's footnotes moves him to say that "footnotes burgeoned and propagated like branches and leaves in a William Morris wallpaper."[28] A lovely comparison that is preceded, however, by a comparison of footnotes to the "impregnably armored bottom" of a tank[29] and succeeded by a scholar who uses a footnote the way "the hockey-masked villain in an American horror film uses a chain saw: to dismember his opponents, leaving their gory limbs scattered across the landscape."[30] The Rabelaisian glee that one feels when thumbing one's nose at the footnote is nicely caught by a

---

24. Anthony Grafton, *The Footnote: A Curious History* (Cambridge, Mass.: Harvard University Press, 1999), p. 5.

25. Ibid.

26. Ibid., p. 6.

27. Ibid., pp. 7–8.

[*] For example, the "low rumble" of the footnote could have been compared to the rumble of drums during an exciting passage of band music. The adjective *nutritious* or *colorful* could have been attached to the fish. And why should the introduction not be a "rambling, enthralling" one?

28. Ibid., p. 111.

29. Ibid., p. 56.

30. Ibid., p. 114.

Noël Coward quip that Grafton joins many other scholars in retelling. "Having to read a footnote," the lyric dramatist claimed, "resembles having to go downstairs to answer the door while in the midst of making love."[31] Scholars, as Coward understood, tend to become infatuated with their prose, though that sometimes astonishes their readers; and so when in the midst of crafting a subtly curving thought, the scholar may very easily feel the footnote is merely an inopportune interruption. That is sad.

The footnote is just as likely to bring to the door a welcome visitor, perhaps handsome or pretty, sometimes garrulous but often pleasantly sociable. Many a somnolent reader has (metaphorically) hugged such a visitor and hoped many more would come to the door: A text sometimes is something only a scholar can love; a footnote, however, is like a blind date, threatening and exciting, dreary occasionally but often entertaining. And a footnote does not require or expect a long-term commitment.

The current climate of opinion of footnotes is ambiguous at best. With the advent of the personal computer, writers find it easier to arrange the "blind date"; publishers can also use the computer to take the guesswork out of the layout. But some writers and publishers have used the Internet as an excuse to eliminate the notes from the published book, offering instead a Web site to which an interested reader can go for the

---

31. Ibid., p. 70. Grafton indicated that three other scholars have used the quip; it can be assumed that many more have passed it along to their doctoral candidates who, scared and lonely as they often are, do not trust any footnote; one can always go wrong and become a dark and menacing stalker, one who doesn't bother to ring the doorbell but clambers into the study through any handy window or by way of a cellar door.

annotations. Virtual reality is a treacherous place, however, filled with black holes and out-of-control meteors; Web sites can go *poof* in a day, a year, a decade, a century. A book then will be left without notes, an argument without documentation, a scholar without credibility. And the relegation of notes to the Internet forecloses any of the dramatic possibility that the footnote's proximity to the text encourages.

Opinion and practice will not be changed simply by pointing out the speciousness of the arguments against the footnote. They will not be changed simply because the footnote has clearly demonstrated its usefulness in the past or because its future holds such promise. They will not be changed simply because scholars, humanists, literate laypersons, and experimental poets[*] have a stake in its continued survival. Appreciation must be informed with knowledge; individual protest must find a common voice. Quite some time ago a scholar called for—in a footnote, of course—"some organization devoted to agitating for the return of footnotes to the place they belong."[32] With the possibility of annotations being rocketed into a virtual space, untended and forgotten, the need for organized agitation is even more pressing. But first we must have a full account of the adventuresome history of the footnote and the many ways it has proved beautiful and desirable. The book is a step in fulfilling that obvious need.

---

[*] See chapter 6, "A Poetic Interlude II."
32. Vincent Tomas, "The Modernity of Jonathan Edwards," *The New England Quarterly*, 10 March 1952, p. 76.

2

The Early Years

THE FIRST FOOTNOTE DRIFTS somewhere in a universe of manuscripts and books, eluding our discovery the way the original bright star of the skies eludes astronomers. But those astronomers have something to teach us: They have not let the vastness of their subject matter discourage them. Sensibly, they made some educated guesses as to the likely conditions that produce stars, then they probed space with telescopes and poked around it with giant radio antennas. And sure enough, they turned up immense, interstellar realms of vast, diffused clouds of gas and dust, *star-forming regions,* within which stars even now are being formed. Observations of these clouds have allowed them to make reasonable guesses as to how the first star must have come into being. And so, if the first star is yet to be found, it still can be described with reasonable accuracy.

We will take our cue from stargazers. Extrapolation is the mind's telescope, and we will use it to reconstruct the beginnings of footnotes. Our *footnote-forming region* will not, of course, be some gas-and-dust cloud in space; it will be in a very human place, where intellectual controversy swirls and where the cut and thrust of argument is most likely to be realized in

a flurry of annotations and commentary. We will assume that
Gutenberg and his first printed books had to appear before
the arrival of the first footnote. Scholars of the Middle Ages
were just as choleric as their later colleagues, but their dis-
agreements, their anger, could be easily expressed in manuscripts by handwritten comments inserted directly into the
text or scrawled in the left or right margins. It was the printed
book that brought a need for order and predictability, space
allocation, and the formal apparatus of reference marks. So
for our likely *footnote-forming region,* we turn to England of the
sixteenth century.

No place was ever more contentious than Elizabethan
London, with its jumble of poets and con artists, smoky
chimneys and church towers, diseases and ideas, with its
masques, sword fights, sonnets, Black Death, with its
William Shakespeare, in whose every couplet order fought
with disorder, its John Donne, whose jostling metaphors
only occasionally succeeded in making sense of his conflicted emotions and contesting ideas, and its Bull, the
Tyburn hangman, a deft hand at cutting a body from the
rope while still alive so as to "open the victim's belly, pull out
his entrails and show them to him before his eyes closed in
death."[1] Bull's brother-in-law was Laurence Pickering, King
of Cutpurses, whose hand was deft at cutting a purse from a
gentleman's body,[2] a nice demonstration of the close relationship of law and order and lawlessness and disorder in
Elizabethan times.

---

1. Gamini Salgado, *The Elizabethan Underworld* (New York: St. Martin's
Press, 1992), p. 11. The narrow focus on criminal life in Salgado's delight-
ful book does not prevent it from giving us a broad and amusing sense
of London life.

2. Ibid., p. 7.

London was a crude place. And it is only by letting this crowded, crime- and disease-ridden city become real to us that we can properly appreciate what thoughtful and fine character was required to create the early footnotes. In the city, sometime before 1568, we can zero in on Richard Jugge, senior Queen's Printer, and give ourselves license to imagine him distractedly strolling the streets, worried sick over a small printed letter, an *f,* cupped between frail slivers of parentheses: (f).

Jugge[3] has been put in charge of printing the Bishops' Bible, a Bible that receives its nickname because it is the bishop-run Church of England's response to the danger-ously popular and subversive Calvinist import, the Geneva Bible. Jugge himself appears to have been a deeply religious soul. He started his career selling books near the north door of St. Paul's under a conspicuous sign picturing a Bible. He then turned to the printing of books, concen-trating first on godly tracts and editions of the New Testament. The Archbishop of Canterbury was fond of him, or at least respected him.

". . . [W]ithout doubt [Jugge] hath well deserved to be pre-ferred," the archbishop was to write when asking the gov-ernment to compensate Jugge for his work on the Bishops' Bible. The job had not been easy, a fact the archbishop rec-ognized when he quickly added: "A man wold not thinke

---

3. For a succinct account of Richard Jugge's life, see Colin Clair, *A History of Printing in Britain* (London: Cassell, 1965), pp. 69–72. References in this book will always give actual page numbers. The term *passim* will not be used to indicate "and pages following." What might seem merely convenient shorthand often conceals information—that is, the amount of attention given to a subject, a fact a reader might need in order to de-cide whether or not to hunt down the reference.

that Jugge had devoured so much pain as he hath sustained."*[4]

Religion could offer comfort to a devout man in the privacy
of his home, and provide companionship and uplift in a
church where people agreed to sing the same hymns, pray the
same prayers, recite the same creed. But in the fierce market
of ideas introduced to Europe by Luther and Calvin and the
Reformation, religion was contentious and dangerous. Voices
were often raised, pamphlets usually scurrilous. A man's head
could be at stake—metaphorically or literally. In etchings and
woodcuts the pope became a three-headed beast, a seven-
headed beast, a demon, the *Anti-Christi;* Luther became a cook
brewing up lies, heresy, unchastity. He morphed into a two-
headed fool, a seven-headed monster, a winesack. The spirit
of *Beavis and Butthead* was afoot. "Luther often spoke of
Germany as the 'papal sow', to be force-fed papal lies for the
pope's sole gain."[5] A woodcut shows the pope holding out a
papal bull; two peasants moon him and fart. Several of
Luther's admirers, offended by a pamphlet put out by the
other side, took turns with it in the men's room and, having
"illustrated" it, returned it to its author.[6]

---

* This quotation has been "translated" in part. In its original it read: "A
man wold not thinke that he had devoured so much payne as he has
susteined." A judgment call: I judged that *wold* and *thinke* would not interrupt the easy flow of a reader, even one new to the Elizabethan era's
ad hoc spellings, whereas *payne* and *susteined* might. And I did not wish
to distract attention from the artful word *devoured;* the archbishop
wants to believe Jugge so devout he was ravenous for the painstaking
work that went into the Bishops' Bible. Let us hope so.

4. *Domestic State Papers. Elizabeth.* vol. XLVIII, 6, in Colin Clair, *A History
of Printing in Britain* (London: Cassell, 1965), p. 71.

5. R. W. Scribner, *For the Sake of Simple Folk: Popular Propaganda for the
German Reformation* (Cambridge, London, New York, New Rochelle,
Melbourne, and Sydney: Cambridge University Press, 1981), p. 82.

6. Ibid., pp. 83–4.

If our Richard Jugge was careless enough to let his stroll take him to London Bridge, he may have shuddered; as many as thirty or thirty-five rotting heads might look down on him from there. Thievery, treason, the wrong faith, or perhaps a sloppy printing job on a Bible might put a man's head on a pike.[7] Bibles were battlefields; their left and right margins were the trenches from which scriptural annotations and citations were lobbed at previous Bibles' misinterpretations: Catholics against Lutherans, Lutherans against Calvinists, Calvinists against the Church of England, and the Church of England against everyone else, and against the noise, the confusion, the lack of decorum. The enormously popular Geneva Bible,* for example, uses Revelation 17:4 to toss a sexually charged grenade at the Pope. Into the text walks a woman "arrayed in purple and skarlat, & guilded with golde, & precious stones, and pearles, [who] had a cup of golde in her hand, full of abominations." The grenade explodes with: "This woman is the Antichrist, that is, the Pope with ye whole bodie of his filthy creatures, . . . whose beauty onely standeth in outwarde pompe & imprudence and craft like a strumpet. . . ."[8]

---

7. Gamini Salgado, *The Elizabethan Underworld* (New York: St. Martin's Press, 1992), p. 1.

* Between 1560 and 1611 there were more than 120 separate editions of the Geneva Bible compared with twenty-two for the Bishops' Bible and only seven for the Great Bible (Henry the Eighth's vain effort to unite his citizens behind a single version of God's word). See Evelyn B. Tribble: *Margins and Marginality: The Printed Page in Early Modern England* (Charlottesville and London: University Press of Virginia, 1993), pp. 31-2.

8. Ibid., p. 35. I remind the reader of my intention to modify Elizabethan spelling; the original reads: ". . . araied in purple and skarlat, & guilded with golde, & precious stones, and pearles, and had a cup of golde in her hand, ful *g* of abominations" and "*f* This woman is the Antichrist, that is, the Pope with ye whole bodie of his filthy creatures, . . . whose beauty onely standeth in outwarde pompe & immprudencie and craft like a strumpet. . . ." Though it may cause difficulty, *guilded* has

The margins of the Geneva Bible could at times look like a muddy cascade of wordy water, tumbling and splashing. On one page the stream of explanation is so great it curls around a corner and pools at the bottom of the page. Someone with less rigorous standards than this author may be tempted to identify this as the first footnote; lacking an independent existence from the margin, however, such overflow is precedent but not fulfillment.

Elizabeth's predecessor, Henry the Eighth, lost his patience with such splashings. Like a talk-show host determined to keep control of discussions that threaten to disintegrate into shouting matches and fisticuffs, the king in 1538 ordered that scripture "in the english tonge" be allowed to speak for itself without "any annotations in the margyn," or for that matter any prologues or additions to calendars and so forth—unless, of course, he approved of them.*

The Bishops' Bible was intended to be as much about decorum as about doctrine. The first edition was handsomely illustrated with engravings, woodcuts, and maps. Dignified portraits of Queen Elizabeth and the earl of Leicester lent weight to the work. Controversy was to be avoided—and also

---

been allowed to stand because this spelling associates *gild* with *guilt* and *guild*. Care must be exercised in the era of Shakespeare and Donne not to drain the words of the full range of their colors simply for the sake of immediate clarity. Reference marks also have been omitted, as they distract and are irrelevant to our purposes.

* Ibid., p. 23. One may suspect that Henry the Eighth might not have been sincere in his quest for orderliness—just as one may suspect Jerry Springer is not always unhappy when his guests raise their voices or their fists. Public insincerity was not unknown to the king; he banned brothels (unsuccessfully), yet he is reputed to have hung a sign over some of the palace's rooms proclaiming MY WHORES' ROOMS—or something to that effect. See Gamini Salgado, *The Elizabethan Underworld* (New York: St. Martin's Press, 1992), p. 41.

private readings by laypersons. It was intended for use of the clergy; paragraph signs red-flagged unsuitable passages, and clergymen were urged to seek out and read other scripture chapters "makying more to [the people's] edification. . . ."[9] Should the laity get their hands on the books, the bishops wanted to be sure there was nothing indiscreet or messy in the margins. Annotations were deliberately "moderate in tone . . . guiding interpretation without invoking the controversy that [might] lie behind the passage."[10] Every other Protestant Bible was tempted to use the book of Revelation to slam the pope. Not this one.

The margins are like carefully constructed, thoughtfully stocked cupboards where good china—but not the finest—waits to be pulled out and used. Nothing glitters but everything is clean and bright.

The day we catch up with Richard Jugge, the book of Job in the Bishops' Bible has been reached. What Jugge may have thought of as the "Geneva Bible problem" is upon him: Annotations threaten to overrun the margins. We should hasten to add that this is probably not his only problem. Jugge in fact might very well have some visceral sympathy with Job; this possibility is worth some extended attention.

Costs were high, his investment great. As yet there was no assurance that he would be granted exclusive rights to the sale of the finished book, and this presented the only possibility of recouping his investment. His workmen were not

9. *The Holie Bible Conteynyng the Olde Testament and the Newe* [Bishops' Bible] (1568), sig. *I[t], in Evelyn B. Tribble, *Margins and Marginality: The Printed Page in Early Modern England* (Charlottesville and London: University Press of Virginia, 1993), p. 38.

10. Evelyn B. Tribble, *Margins and Marginality: The Printed Page in Early Modern England* (Charlottesville and London: University Press of Virginia, 1993), p. 43.

necessarily reliable. Though no direct evidence of his employees' habits is available, historians and economists have been quick to make judgments about the general attitudes of workmen at the time. One of them writes: "The English laborer . . . responded when prices fell or wages rose, so that he could satisfy his wants with diminished effort, by keeping holiday the remainder of his time." (References in this paragraph will be grouped together in a footnote at the end of the paragraph. An explanation for this delay is made there.) A commentator, Thomas Manly, closer in time to Jugge (1669), noted: "They work so much fewer days by how much the more they exact in wages. . . ." A harsher (and anonymous) comment was made in 1728: "People in low life who work only for their daily bread, if they can get it by three days work in a week will many of them make holiday the other three or set their own price on their labour." D. F. McKenzie speculates that early printers may sometimes have preferred apprentices to journeymen precisely because apprentices could be ordered to work and journeymen could not. "Such an argument was in fact used in litigation in 1592 [twenty-four years after the first Bishops' Bible appeared] when Benjamin Prince, a journeyman . . . said he need only do what he could whereas Parker, an apprentice had to do as his master bade him."[11]

---

11. Most of the time the convenience of the reader dictates that each separate citation be given a separate footnote. This paragraph is an exception. All of the diverse citations come to me from a single source: D. F. McKenzie, "Printers of the Mind: Some Notes on Bibliographical Theories and Printing-House Practices," *Studies in Bibliography,* vol. 22, 1969. This grouping of citations alerts the reader to the fact that I make no claim to original research, a claim that a trail of footnotes through the paragraph might make unwittingly. The references in order of appearance: 1. E. S. Furniss, *The Position of the Laborer in a System of Nationalism* (1920), p. 234: see McKenzie, note 15, p. 11. (McKenzie asserts

One rightly may be suspicious of an argument that attributes tardiness and absenteeism solely to the fickleness of employees. A hundred good reasons can excuse someone's absence: a wife in labor, a mother dying, a child gone missing, a squabble with a landlord, fear of a plague or of a witch, a broken foot, a cold (especially in the damp London winters), and so forth. Even D. F. McKenzie admits the discussion must be related to what we know of journeymen's grievances. "It may be that under conditions of widespread unemployment an increase in part-time work is to be expected rather than a severe restriction of the labour force to the few men of highest efficiency."* Whatever the reasons, workmen for whom we happen to have production figures show widely

---

in the footnote: "The contemporary evidence cited by Furniss is full and detailed.") 2. For Thomas Manly see D. C. Coleman, "Labour in the English Economy of the 17th Century," *Economic History Review,* 2nd ser. VIII (1956), pp. 280–95: McKenzie, note 15, p. 11. 3. For "anonymous," see *Some Thoughts on the Interest of Money,* cited by Furniss. 4. For Benjamin Prince, see "Notes on Printing at Cambridge, c. 1590," trans. Cambridge Bibliographical Society III (1959), p. 102: McKenzie, note 17, p. 11. McKenzie's introductory comments appear in note 17.

* Academics and workmen may lack understanding of each other. Every so often I have heard one faculty member complain to another about the amount of time custodians or electricians or security guards or—less often—student dishwashers spend just standing around "doing nothing," this while standing around waiting for a meeting or a class or lunch to start. It seems to escape them that work requiring hands and backs also can require the planning and coordinated efforts that necessitate standing around and talking. Workmen, of course, often show a reciprocal disdain for academics. Talking to students, lecturing, writing and reading, staring off into space in search of an idea do not look like "real work." I sometimes tell them that a study once compared occupations and calorie expenditure; writers proved to have used up more calories per hour than longshoremen. Disbelief is the usual reaction and, because I cannot "access" the study, the disbelief usually remains. Both sides misunderstand each other's work, I think, but as academics write

varying degrees of diligence. In 1702 Thomas Pokins, a compositor at the University of Cambridge press, set type at an exceptional rate: an average of 6,307 characters a day. His colleagues' averages were well behind. A William Bertram composed 5,700 a day; one Clement Knell did just 5,603 on an average day.[12]

Pay was tied to production, ensuring fits of jealousy, backstabbing, maybe even subtle forms of sabotage. (I write from personal experience on this matter. As the supervisor of an all-female assembly line paid piecework wages for assembling fluorescent lights, I witnessed acts of sabotage and retaliation. One assembler hoarded parts, hiding them from her colleagues—and from me. All had fits of anger, some tossed things—occasionally at me—as the pressure to produce squeezed them into harridans entirely different from the people they were outside of work. On the street they always waved and hallooed to me pleasantly. I do not believe sixteenth-century workers would be much different from their modern-day counterparts in this regard.) One has to believe Jugge had personnel problems weighing on him most days.

And he must have had personal problems as well. As he walks along the Thames we cannot have him simply worrying about wages and absenteeism and the overcrowded margins of Job. The intense odors of garbage and offal, dumped unceremoniously into the street by every homeowner, the scav-

---

much more about workers than workers write about academics, the former lend permanence to their errors and bear a heavier responsibility to generalize with care. See D. F. McKenzie, "Printers of the Mind: Some Notes on Bibliographical Theories and Printing-House Practices," *Studies in Bibliography,* vol. 22, 1969, note 17, p. 11.

12. D. F. McKenzie, "Printers of the Mind: Some Notes on Bibliographical Theories and Printing-House Practices," *Studies in Bibliography,* vol. 22, 1969, p. 9.

enging kites swooping down to dine, also must be allowed to distract him. We will give him the sniffles. And because we can, we will let him scan the city's horizon. London was then a low-lying, horizontal city with St. Paul's (a stubby, inelegant early version of the present-day cathedral) and the Tower of London reaching up and calling attention to themselves. These last two were reminders of church and government that he does not particularly welcome this day, we presume. Several criminals tied up by the riverside will add a nice touch, and a passing chimney sweep's cry: "Sweep chimney sweep mistress, with a hey derry sweep from the bottom to top, sweep chimney sweep." But amid the noise and smells and dangers, the (f) and the (g) nag him like a persistent cough.*

Space is the problem. Half of the first page of the book of Job is taken up by titles and by an elaborate illustration of a semi-naked man receiving counsel from four fashionably

---

* Historians are always suspicious of the kind of "color commentary" supplied in this paragraph. Assertions that are not based on firm evidence or, at least, derived from a plausible argument are not admitted to Clio's noisy court. And this author readily admits there is no evidence Jugge saw, smelled, or thought what is attributed to him, nor that he worried or sniffled on the day he arrived at a solution for the overcrowded margin. However, to present the invention of the footnote as if it were achieved in a disembodied mind, a vacuum, would also be a distortion. We must not let our admiration for the abstract acrobatics of brilliant minds allow us to overlook the pull, the dragging down of daily life. Thought must contend with gravity sooner or later. Einstein had to have his wisdom teeth pulled. Newton once in a while must have had a runny nose, a sore throat. Charles Dickens took long compulsive walks and hid out with a mistress. We know for a fact that Archimedes took baths. Their genius was to defy gravity, not escape it. If the particular details we have supplied Jugge hang on him like a misfitted suit, well, we mustn't let him walk the streets naked. He must be seen to have invented the footnote with his feet on the ground and his head filled with distractions if we are to honor him properly.

dressed men whose helmets and turbans bloom on their head like orchids. Seven notes need to be accommodated on the left margin. Five, (a), (b), (c), (d), and (e), can be accommodated by starting the (a) to the side of and halfway down the illustration, an awkward intrusion into the decorated space but tolerable. The (f) and the (g) are left orphans, however. The solution found in the Geneva Bible, the curling of the notes into the bottom of the page, had to be rejected by Jugge; the disorder of that Bible was just what the bishops had instructed him to avoid. The answer Jugge came up with was, like many of the advances made in book design over the years, subtle: (f) and (g) did end up on the bottom of the page, but a small, meaningful space was left between them and their descending companions. Avoided was any appearance that (f) and (g) had been shoved into their place; instead, like sunbathers on a crowded beach who manage to set themselves off from the others by carefully placing their blanket to one side (and perhaps by adopting a certain sang froid), the notes at the bottom of the page appear to have the space solely to themselves. They bring the exclusivity of the Hamptons to Jones Beach. Jugge, snapping his fingers perhaps, has found a way to include an abundance of notes yet maintain decorum.

Could Jugge have managed it, greater separation between notes would have been even more pleasing; (f) and (g) jostle each other inappropriately. Those reservations aside, Jugge stands in the streets of London as a plausible candidate for the person who first conceived the idea of a footnote.* Much

---

* Just as astronomers know that earlier and earlier stars will be found, we expect someday our research will be superseded by the discovery of an earlier footnote. The exploration of the bottom of early book pages should be encouraged. This author with the cooperation of Invisible Cities Press is offering a modest but appropriate recognition for the discoverer of a qualified footnote that appears in history prior to the (f),

work must be done, however, before the *idea* of (f) could become a physical object in the world of men and books and London smog. Let us follow it into the pressure cooker of a sixteenth-century printing house.

The typefoundry would be the place where the (f) got its start. A 1568 illustration of a typefoundry shows a cube of a furnace perhaps two feet by four feet, and perhaps four feet high.[13] An open hole on its side invites logs to be tossed into it. A large bellows leans against the wall, looking a bit worn— as if it had been used too often and wanted simply to slide to the floor, stretch out, and rest. A basket for wood is nearly empty. A rather uncomfortably dressed man sits on a hard-looking metal block in front of the furnace. At his feet is a basket of finished type. Large windows strike a pleasant note but, remarkably, no chimney can be seen.

The typefounder appears calm and unworried, though we know any fire was a lurking hazard. Houses were built close together, combustible materials collected in homes and were tossed out into the alleys, chimneys—when there were chimneys—were often wood! Fire-fighting techniques were primitive. A bucket brigade might form. Snow, manure, vinegar, damp cloths, urine were all used to squelch the flames.[14] A Nehemiah Wellington reported that in 1626 a small blaze was discovered in his home; his apprentice and servant quickly

---

and which is used in any future edition of this book: A footnote will record the name of the discoverer, who will be given a celebratory dinner at a restaurant of his or her choice for up to one hundred dollars.

13. Michael Clapham, "Printing," *A History of Technology,* vol. III, ed. Charles Singer et al. (Oxford: Clarendon Press, 1957), p. 391.

14. Penny Roberts, "Agencies Human and Divine: Fire in French Cities, 1520–1720," *Fear in Early Modern Society,* ed. William G. Naphy and Penny Roberts (Manchester and New York: Manchester University Press, 1997), p. 13.

"pissed out the fire."[15] A more effective measure for large con-
flagrations was to pull down the houses in its path in hopes
of starving the fire; but "the rapid demolition of any building
was no easy or quick task, and careful calculation had to be
made regarding the speed and direction of the fire, inevitably
provoking the antagonism of any whose house was condemned as a result."[16] The response to London's Great Fire of
1666 was slow perhaps because the Lord Mayor was reluctant
to offend wealthy homeowners. (He reportedly minimized
the fire, saying "Pish, a woman might piss it out."[17]) The
foundry furnace would not be a welcome addition to the
neighborhood, presumably. In Troyes, France, in fact, a fur-
bisher tried to get a printer evicted because "for the last two
weeks fires had been lit at night."[18]

It is unlikely the (f) was made as a single piece of type; instead, the (, the f, and the) would have been made separately
so as to allow their use in other combinations.[19] The typefounder thus has his work cut out for him. A hair-thin sliver
of moon, the (, is dug into the end of a bar of steel. The steel
is heated to cherry-red, then plunged into water or oil to

---

15. Christopher R. Friedrichs, *The Early Modern City 1450–1750* (London
and New York: Longman, 1995), p. 278.

16. Penny Roberts, "Agencies Human and Divine: Fire in French
Cities, 1520–1720," *Fear in Early Modern Society,* ed. William G. Naphy
and Penny Roberts (Manchester and New York: Manchester University
Press, 1997), p. 14.

17. Friedrichs, ibid., p. 278.

18. Roberts, ibid., p. 22.

19. E. Rayher of Northfield, Massachusetts, a present-day printer experienced in the use of small presses and in the casting of type, assures me
that the cost of type at that time would justify the added difficulty of
separate casts for each element of the (f). Admittedly, he made his observations using a microfilm copy of the Bible, and so his opinion is not to
be taken as conclusive.

harden it; the steaming and hissing must have turned heads. Heated a second time, its tip a bright straw color now, the steel is tempered, cooled, and driven hard into a bar of copper, imprinting the tiny right parenthesis. This imprint, or matrix, as it is called, is fixed firmly to a mold. The typefounder now holds it upside down. The mold has a funnel-like entrance into which he can pour the hot type metal. This entrance will leave a telltale protrusion attached to the finished type that came to be known as the tang.

An odd-shaped ladle of lead compound has been sitting on the top of the furnace long enough for the lead to become a dangerously hot liquid. As we watch, our typefounder lifts and twists and thrusts the ladle toward the mold, a practiced gesture requiring agility and timing. A gob of hot lead slides along the tang, floods through a tiny hole, and enters the body of the mold. The lead splashes into the copper (. Enough force has been imparted to the lead by the curious motion of the typefounder that every bit of the minute line of curve is filled. Cooling is almost instantaneous for the small type. The mold is opened; a new piece of type drops out into the basket.

A small girl, eight or nine, enters the picture.* We ought to let such a youngster daydream a bit, though her dreams will not be those our own children would have. *Witches:* she has grown up with stories about "cunning men" and "wise women," "conjurors" *(sic)* and "sorcerers," "blessers" and "charmers." They were people to treasure as well as fear. They could charm away a toothache, find a lost purse or a straying sheep, make corn grow tall, a man fall in love, a hoarse voice warble like a bird. They could predict the weather or the sex

* Young boys were usually employed for this work, but a girl was not unknown.

of a yet-to-be-born child, cure a disease or exorcise a demon by measuring a girdle or by releasing a live bat in the sickroom or by boiling a lock of the afflicted's hair.[20] It was an era when Harry Potter lived next door and the Wicked Witch of the West was down the street. A child did not need Saturdaymorning television to find magic and adventure; she simply needed to listen to the adults talk. Let's require of history that she has heard the instructions of Thomas Ross: "How to walk on the water, a proper secret: . . . take two little timbrels and bind them under the soles of thy feet, and at a stave's end fasten another, and with these you may safely walk on the water unto the wonder of all . . . if . . . you . . . exercise the same with a certain boldness and lightness of the body."[21] With those instructions in her head, she scoops up the basket of type. As she carries it over to her seat, she is tiptoeing across a gentle stream (not the dangerous Thames) while a brother stranded on the bank stamps his foot with envy. The water and timbrels splash and thrum in a common rhythm.

Seated, she must take a piece of type between her fingers and snap off the tang—a motion repeated again and again. She does not notice the slight prick the tang gives her,* for now she is sitting on the far side of the stream watching her brother struggle to wade across.

The type (is soon deposited in a type case, a box of compartments within which the type, segregated by kind, waits to

---

20. Gamini Salgado, *The Elizabethan Underworld* (New York: St. Martin's Press, 1992), p. 78.

21. Thomas Ross, *Natural and Artificial Conclusions* (1567), in ibid., p. 75.

* See the *Oxford English Dictionary:* "Tang . . . I. 1. A projecting pointed part or instrument. a. The tongue of a serpent formerly thought to be the stinging organ. . . ." E. Rayher assures me that type once removed from the mold cools quickly. A child's fingers would not be burned; but the tang's rough edge could prick a daydreaming child.

be plucked out by a compositor. Composing type requires speed and accuracy of a high order; it is skilled labor. This day the compositor plucks with tweezers* the piece of type on which rests the parenthesis. His fingers grab it; they feel for a notch that tells them the type is right-side up. The wrist flicks the (into position on the composing stick, a nifty handheld device, the size of a very large comb, which nestles lines of type and keeps them secure. The wrist tweezers pluck again instantly, the fingers squeeze, the wrist flicks, and (f appears in the composing stick. Then (f). The reference mark for the first footnote has been assembled. But the job is not yet done.

Our composer works in a very busy and noisy room. Ten workers are shown in a 1590 illustration.[22] The printing press is banging away, the printer straining. A dignified, worried man points a finger at some copy and instructs one of the two compositors, who ignores him and continues with his work. A ladder leans against the wall near a window as if someone had just been up it fixing a leak. A couple of proofreaders are peering suspiciously, one scanning a proof, another redoing some set type. Someone comes in with additional type balanced on his head. Someone else spreads ink across type. And off in one corner the head of the establishment extends an open hand, like the patron in a religious painting whose money has bought him the chance to be included in the picture as the one pointing to a miracle—or martyrdom.

The miracle is our compositor's concentration as he slides in tiny lead spacers. They ensure that the (f) is at the right height

---

* Tweezers were called botkins; specialized printing terminology has been avoided when possible. Annotation, not the printed book, is our subject; printers enter only because they are necessary to a full understanding of the wonder of the first footnote.

22. Michael Clapham, "Printing," *A History of Technology*, vol. III, ed. Charles Singer et al. (Oxford: Clarendon Press, 1957), p. 395.

above and distance from the larger *t* that proceeds it and the *a* that follows it. (The sentence in the text in which (f) appears is: "And when the dayes of their banquetting were gone about, Job sent (f) and sanctified them, and gat up early and (g) offered for every one a burnt offering: for Job saide. . . ."[23] and continues for a while. A sentence the compositor may well have felt he had been sentenced to.)

The Bishops' Bible with its relatively few notes must have been welcomed initially. But if margin notes irritated a conscientious compositor, this new footnote thing must have been a torment. The (f) needed extra pieces of lead under each part to lift it up to its correctly lofty place between the other larger letters. The chances of the compositor dropping such tiny pieces had to make him nervous. He was slowed up; the risk of error was increased; and the note itself had to be fitted into the page bottom, no sure thing. That it was followed by a second footnote (g), and that both came just as the trials of Job got under way, surely made him bite his lip: Was this a sign of more footnote tribulations to come? Children aren't the only ones to believe in omens.

Briefly we give our compositor pleasure by letting him think of all the other lucrative trades requiring coordination and agile hands he might engage in. A cutpurse, perhaps, who spots Richard Jugge (assuming Jugge is held responsible for the footnotes). The compositor/cutpurse falls to the floor as if in a swoon; Jugge, religious but also kind, goes to the poor man's aid. He bends over; his purse dangles; he utters soothing words. Only after the fainted man's recovery, the flurry of

---

23. *The Holie Bible* [microform] (London: Richard Jugge . . . [1568]), pagination unreadable. The first footnote is on the first page of the book of Job; *fent, fanctified,* and *faide,* in the original, have been changed to *sent, sanctified,* and *saide.*

thanks, the hurried departure for a doctor's appointment does Jugge feel for an absent purse. Or Jugge gambles, admittedly an unlikely event except in fantasy. The compositor/ cony catcher joins the card game, Mumchance, which has lured the printer. Jugge is allowed as if by chance to see a king of hearts, a card near the top of the pack. When the several gamblers name a card, Jugge, of course, names the king of hearts, and when the deck is dealt the king is the first of the named cards to appear. He wins the pot. A second and a third time he gets his advance look and he wins. Now he throws into the pot all his money; he has spotted the jack of hearts, a fickle lover but a sure bet. The cards are dealt. One . . . two . . . three . . . four. The jack should have shown. Five . . . six . . . Another gambler cries: "Mine" and scoops up the pot.[24]

The compositor/cony catcher does not get to split up the conned money because now he must carefully slide the lines of type in his composing stick into the "chase." The chase holds completed pages of type, and must be adjusted with wooden strips so margins and pages are properly spaced and firmly held in the frame. Our compositor, we assume, sighed with relief when the first page of the book of Job was hustled away.

The heavy chase of type is inked, lifted, and tugged under a hinged "frisket." The frisket looks somewhat like a large waffle iron. The inked type pokes up from the bottom; the paper lies across it; a protective batten lies on the paper; and the top is closed, holding everything in place. The frisket is slid into the printing press as if into an oven—though the press will assault it with force instead of heat. The pressman, his legs braced, the muscles of his arms bulging, pulls the press lever with a quick, sharp jerk. His weight and strength travel along

---

24. See Gamini Salgado, *The Elizabethan Underworld* (New York: St. Martin's Press, 1992), p. 26, for details.

the lever, increasing as they go, enter a massive screw, and, circling and circling, pick up further steam. (A screw can be
thought of as just a lever that has been twisted to save space.
To have exerted the same force at the end of a straight lever,
the pressman might have had to stand on the other side of the
Thames or farther.) The screw drives a flat board hard onto
the frisket. Bang. The paper is crushed against bristling type.

Violent force is necessary. Paper of that era was not the artificial, easily penetrable stuff of our time. Put our paper under
a microscope and you see straight grains, regular as Kansas
corn rows. Elizabethan paper was made of pulped rag that refused to be regular; rather, it was tangled and at cross purposes like an overgrown thicket that defies a path. The ink had
to drive into that thicket in order to imprint: (f) That is, he
willed the[m] to be sanctified, in abstaining fro[m] carnal appetites, and showed how they should behave them selves
holylie and soberlie in their banquettes. (g) Herein is Jobs religion and feare of God knowen, & the fatherly care of his children expressed.[25] The printer would be less than human if he
did not wish in his heart of hearts for an abstention from tiny,
easily blotted footnotes rather than from carnal appetites.

An incident at the time of a later edition of the Bishops'
Bible is worth noting. Perhaps to save money, the edition did
away with some of the more lavish illustrations. To compensate, the press borrowed 114 decorated initials that made "a
profuse display."[26] One used to start Saint Paul's exceedingly
proper epistle to the Hebrews in which all sinners are threat-

---

25. *The Holie Bible* [microform] (London: Richard Jugge . . . [1568]), pagination unreadable. The first footnote is in the first page of the book of
Job. (Minor changes in spelling have been made.)

26. Colin Clair, *A History of Printing in Britain* (London: Cassell, 1965),
pp. 71–2.

ened with eternal damnation (fornicators in particular) turned out to represent Leda and the Swan.

A most incongruous decoration, the incongruity made vivid to later readers of Yeats: ". . . Above the staggering girl, her thighs caressed / By the dark webs, her nape caught in his bill, / He holds her helpless breast upon his breast. . . ." No one at Jugge's press, not the compositors, nor the pressmen, nor the "correctors," brought Leda to his attention; Jugge was "severely censured."[27] Did the workers at Jugge's press refuse to mimic the acquiescence of Job? Did the added work of the first footnotes cause them to rebel? Is it stretching the evidence to believe that antagonism to the first footnote may have led to this early Luddite action? Caution says yes, it is too much; the lust for historical irony, however, demands we make the leap of faith.

The footnote, like any other significant invention, begins as an idea in someone's swirling gray matter, then seeks a way through human distractions, daydreams, fantasies, arguments, and conflicts, and then gets itself transformed into a "thing." Our (f) was turned into a scratch on hot iron and a depression in copper, then rode on the top of a mold and was slid and pushed into a line of type. It was slathered by ink and, finally, it had paper slammed against it. Now it rides the paper in the Bishops' Bible, does a complicated dance with light waves and our eyes, and once again is a trace of an idea fluttering across gray matter. If we forget the long trek of the footnote, as writers, readers, and thinkers are apt to, some of the wonder and joy of creation disappear.

To return to outer space for a comparison, the sun is such a familiar object we scarcely think of it for days at a time, and

---

27. Ibid, pp. 71-2.

when we stop to watch a sunset or sunrise, we are unlikely to remember its history: the explosions of gas and dust eons ago that produced this miracle. Harried scholars, eyes squinting in the fluorescent light of some library's stacks, are even less likely to think of the unique wonder of the footnote's journey to their mind, but their search would have more zest and "truth" if they did.

We need to guard the concept of invention against another common distortion. Take the airplane, for example. We often say casually that the Wright brothers "invented the airplane," and the word *airplane* these days unpacks a sleepy Lindbergh crossing the Atlantic, British pilots scrambling into Spitfires, a Chuck Yeager breaking the sound barrier, and the SST becoming a commonplace to the very wealthy and to crossword puzzle devotees. This *airplane* contains a series of inventions and a multitude of inventors and heroes who can be admitted without diminishing the splendor of Kitty Hawk and the tiny biplane that fluttered a few feet that spring day in 1903.

But failures should also be present in any successful "invention." The oversized wood-and-paper wings early pilots strapped to their chests and frantically beat the air with, the lumbering machines that never got off the ground or fell like rocks off the side of a cliff, all the strange contraptions that ended as tangled heaps are as much a part of the invention of the airplane as the successes. (In some areas of science we are accustomed to the usualness and need of failed experiments; it is part of the serious daily work of a physicist or chemist. Failure in technology can be too easily a visual comedy, a pratfall, and lead to a dismissal of its necessity in the inventive process.) For the footnote, too, failure is an integral part of its progress; we will keep that in mind.

Jugge's footnote was a convenience; it was not yet a research tool or humanizing aside. In the years that followed, the English establishment seems to have corralled margin notes as if they were stampeding cows and stamped out footnotes as if noxious weeds. Neatness was everything. A book of biographies of English kings written by William Martyn, Esq., and printed by James Boler in 1628 can represent any number of tidy printings of the post-Jugge era.

The title page of the Boler book gives the game away. A Roman archway attempts to be gay and voluptuous: vines heavy with grapes and broad leaves circle the twin columns; an odd pairing—a bemused lion and a contented unicorn— appear opposite each other at the spring line. Behind them, a thorny rose and bristling thistle thrust and curl to the top, where a jeweled crown rests on the keystone like a keystone itself. The title is more reserved than the expansive rule of its time: *The Historie and Lives of the Kings of England: From William the Conqueror, unto the end of the Raigne of King Henry the Eighth. With other useful observations.*[28] Everything is in a container: the title in the archway, the flowers and animals within severe borders. The effect is a repressed sensuality seldom associated with the irrepressible royalty that is the subject of the book; it is as if Martyn is insisting *he* rules over Henry the Eighth and company, not they over him.

This emotional tightfistedness is confirmed by the introduction. "Worthie Gentlemen (omitting all elaborated Eloquence which oftentimes is used as a varnish to cover unprofitable labours; As cunning Goldsmithes doe enrich their

---

28. William Martyn, *The Historie and Lives of the Kings of England. From William the Conqueror, unto the end of the Raigne of King Henry the Eighth* (London: James Boler, 1628), unpaginated. *F*'s have been changed to *S*'s when appropriate; *account* is *accompt* in the original.

basest Silver, when they Gilt it with their purest Gold) I purpose to render to you an account of two reasons, which in-
duced mee to take this paine, and to publish this worke."[29]
The containment within parentheses of an eloquent rejection
of elaborate eloquence shows Martyn at his slyest, a deliberate craftsman of repression.*

    This tactic may be less well advised further into the work.
The text is bordered on the left and at the bottom by a thin,
tight line—no room is provided for even the tiniest note. (One
can almost see Martyn's equally thin smile as he persuades
Boler to add the lines or, alternatively, he hears his publisher
suggest them.) On the right are two such insistent lines an
inch apart; they are elevator shafts.

    Page after page goes by with no traffic up or down the shaft,
just emptiness. When one does finally appear, at page 191, for example, the results are frustrating. Martyn has gotten us to

---

29. Ibid., Epistle Dedica`torie [sic], unpaginated.

* Sometimes the effort to contain margin notes and repress footnotes
is even more obviously connected to the issue of maintaining law and
order in an age of exuberance and gunpowder. A dismal treatise on the
laws of Moses by John Weemes jumps to mind. Weemes should have
been saved by providence for our current era, when he would have served
splendidly in traffic court; he delights in minutiae and in the pounding
of a gravel. A right-hand column appears in the pages of his book but
is used solely for emphasis, never for amplification. No footnotes are
allowed, of course. While detailing lawful ceremonies, Weemes confronts
a biblical text in which "Lions, Oxen & Cherubims" appear. The
cherubims make him nervous. He immediately describes an elaborate
system of wings. Wings cover their faces and feet. Two wings stretch
out to cover whatever is in between. The text tells us "the Lord would
not have them to appeare naked. . . ." And the margin note echoes
shrilly, "The Lord would have the Cherubims covered and not to appeare
naked." A cigar is sometimes a cigar but this kind of excess of decorum
registers as almost certainly more than merely an excess of decorum. See
John Weemes, *An Exposition of the Lawes of Moses* (no city given: J. Dawson,
F. J. Bellamie, 1632), p. 36.

France as its royalty gears up for battle with Henry the Fifth and his archers. Money is in short supply. Charles, the dauphin, with help from the high constable of France, weasels from his mother, the queen, "a great Masse of silver and of gold, which for many yeares she had scraped, scratched, and hoarded up together."[30] The queen is inwardly "enraged" and plans "to bee revenged"[31] but she apparently does not refuse. Can she not say no to her son? The reader stops, stands there motionless as if waiting for an elevator door to open. The door opens to a closed-mouth repetition: "She voweth deep revenge."[32]

The ruling out (in a literal sense) of footnotes and even of margin notes that add rather than just repeat is a common occurrence during this period. But there are also small outbreaks of rebellion; the English after the death of Elizabeth the First were not obstreperous just as subjects but as writers too.

Some of the rebellious notes are simply the broken china or spilled drink of passionate speech at a tea. In 1613, for example, Roger Widdrington, an English Catholic, tosses his drink into the air. This is startling because Widdrington appears to be usually a restrained, meticulous man, the kind of person who unobtrusively straightens pictures if they lean to one side and goes for water if an elder or a vase of fresh flowers seems in need. Again the title page says it all; it is thorough and thoughtful at the risk of being long-winded: "A Theologicall Disputation Concerning the Oath of Allegiance, dedicated to the most Holy Father Pope Paul *the fifth*, Wherein All The Principall arguments which have hitherto beene brought by Cardinall *Bellarmine, Leonard Leffius, Martin*

---

30. William Martyn, *The Historie and Lives of the Kings of England: From William the Conqueror, unto the end of the Raigne of King Henry the Eighth* (London: James Boler, 1628), p. 191.

31. Ibid.

32. Ibid.

Becanus, and divers others, against the new *Oath of Allegiance,*
lately established in England by Act of Parliament, are sincerely, *perspicuously, and exactly examined."* Widdrington
catches his breath and, still not satisfied, adds: "Translated
out of Latin into English by the Author himselfe, where unto
hee hath also added *An Appendix,* wherein all the arguments,
which the most learned Divine *Franciscus Surarez,* hath lately
brought for the Popes power to depose Princes, and against
the aforesaid *Oath of Allegiance,* are sincerely rehearsed, and
answered."[33] The pages that follow reflect the neat and judicious temperament of Widdrington. He chooses his words
with care, balances his sentences, uses italics and capitals
sparingly and appropriately for emphasis. Though lined margins on both sides of the text are available for notes, he uses
them judiciously. He provides no space at all at the bottom of
the page for notes. He would have thought none necessary.

But by page 45, the fierce dispute between Anglicans and
Roman Catholics and the terrible weight of religious and political responsibility bring this dignified and considerate man
to a fighting pitch. A suggestion that "some worthie men,
among whom some also were Popes"[34] so distresses him that
his response spills over in to the left margin and the note,
churning and foaming, tumbles down to the bottom, a water-
fall of choler. It has no choice but to force its way back under
the text: welling passion undermining reasoned argument.

---

33. Roger Widdrington, *A Theologicall Disputation Concerning the Oath of
Allegiance, dedicated to the most Holy Father Pope Paul* the fifth, *Wherein All
The Principall arguments which have hitherto beene brought by Cardinall*
Bellarmine, Leonard Leffius, Martin Becanus, *and divers others, against the
new* Oath of Allegiance, *lately established in England by Act of Parliament, are
sincerely,* perspicuously, and exactly examined (London[?]: E. Allde[?],
1613), unpaginated.

34. Ibid., p. 45.

Poor John Rainolds, another writer at a different time, comes to be equally incensed. His objections to the public stage earned him letters of "reprove" from a Mr. Gager, and a copy of that gentleman's new "Trageie *[sic]*"—one presumes this last the more offensive communication. Though his text turns harsh at times, it strives to be considerate of others' feelings. In previous correspondence Rainolds has advanced the argument that stage plays waste money better spent to aid the poor.

The money spent on plays would never reach the poor in any case is the reply; the money presumably would go for gambling or fine clothes or the funding of armadas. A case in point is given: Nero, who "being tickled with desire of praise; and loving to heare men approve his playing on the stage with clapping of their hands, and crying out, *Excellent, Excellent,* did choose a lusty band of valiant youths to doe it, whole captianes he gave three hundred pound a piece, or better"[35]—not money, however, that Nero would have directed to good works. "Waste is waste," Rainolds in effect is reduced to arguing, and his frustration spills out into thirteen sputtering Latin notes in the margin and at the bottom of the page.[36] A confusion of reference marks betrays his agitation: d, e, f, *, d, *, e, f, g, h, i, *, l. Further along Rainolds, the classicist, so

---

35. John Rainolds, *The OVERTHROW OF STAGEPLAYES By the way of controversie betwixt D. Gager and D. Rainoldes* [sic], *wherein all the reasons that can be made for them are notably refuted; the observations answered, and the case fo[r] cleared and resolved, at what the judgement of any man, that is not forward and perverse, may easilie bee satisfied. WHEREIN IS MANIFESTLY proved that it is not onely unlawfull to be an Actor but a beholder of those vanities* (Oxford: John Lichfield, 1629), p. 25. *F*'s are changed to *S*'s, *U*'s to *V*'s.

36. Ibid., p. 52. The note is a long, nervous explanation of why Rainolds had the audacity to insert a word in one of his citings of Gager's letter. ". . . I take the omitting thereof . . . to be a slippe of your penne, and therefore doe insert it." At just this point the margin gives out; the note curls into something that resembles a respectful bow. (*F*'s changed to *S*'s.)

loses control of himself that he breaks out with an occasional note in English.

Sixteen hundred twenty-nine was a watershed year in British history: Charles the First dissolved Parliament, a first step down a path that soon brought him face to face with Oliver Cromwell, and which twenty years later put his head under the ax. The year will serve as well as any other to mark the end of the early era of the footnote. Like the English people, the footnote was in for tumultuous times, days that tested people's values and set one against the other. Without overdramatizing the role of the footnote in political and social history, we can claim for it some importance in the working out of the seventeenth and eighteenth centuries' values. It became a field of battle on which—perhaps with more clarity than on the fields where Cromwell and Charles the First fought—exuberance tested restraint, exploration assaulted stay-at-homeness, and fecundity lay siege to tidiness.

3

A Poetic Interlude

THE EXHILARATION WE FEEL when suddenly coming upon a fecund (if tangled) garden of scholarly notes should not keep us from registering how dark were the surrounding woods where the footnote of poetry wandered throughout the seventeenth century and into the eighteenth. In that wood of spies and feuds and character assassins, the footnote was waylaid and mugged. The mugger, a professional, was Alexander Pope; his weapon *The DUNCIAD VARIORUM with the PROLEGOMENA of SCRIBLERUS,* a poem stuffed with satirical comments and remarks like an old sock with rocks. It is a devious story.

We pick up the trail in France, in the 1640s, at the court of the exiled English king. Abraham Cowley prepares to return to England as a royalist spy. He is "advis'd to dissemble the main Intention of his coming over, under the Disguise of applying himself to some settled Profession." That of "Physick" is "thought most proper."[1] He makes his way to a "fruitful part of Kent" fully intending (we can suppose) to follow instructions. The profusion of herbs, bushes, and trees he finds in Kent, however, seduces him; he becomes a gardener and

---

1. Janet Todd, ed., *The Works of Aphra Behn,* vol. 1 (Columbus: Ohio State University Press, 1992), p. 443.

poet, occupations that do not make quite as effective a cover story as physician, perhaps, but which seem to have served.* What role his secret work played in the eventual defeat of Cromwell and the restoration of the English monarchy is difficult to judge. Not difficult to judge is his poetry, which brings us pleasure as it also brings us an elaborate apparatus of notes. His cautious placement of them at the end of the poem rather than at the foot of the page (which appears to be still a somewhat controversial positioning in those days) is understandable; a secret agent, risking his head for king and country, surely has an incentive to act timidly in other parts of his life.

We can pause only for a few examples of his work. *Davideis, a Sacred Poem of the Troubles of David in Four Books,* begins with a traditional "proposition":

> I Sing the *Man* who *Judahs Scepter* bore
> In that right hand which held the Crook before;
> Who from the best Poet, best of Kings did grow;
> The two chief gifts Heav'n could on Man bestow.[2]

The very first line inspires two notes. The second one—a thorough explanation of his substitution of *Judah* for the more expected *Israel*—will be passed over; but the first note is a gem. It exhibits the mix of pride and humility that so be-

---

* Cowley's biographer, Thomas Sprat, betrays some annoyance with Cowley's failure to employ his gardening skills "for Practice and Profit" but instead "presently digested it into the Form which we behold. . . ." The bottom line, though, is that his spying remained a secret. See Janet Todd, ed., *The Works of Aphra Behn,* vol. 1 (Columbus: Ohio State University Press, 1992), p. 443.

2. Abraham Cowley, *Poems: Miscellanies, The Mistress, Pindarique Odes, Davideis. Verses Written on Several Occasions* (Cambridge: Cambridge University Press, 1905), p. 251.

comes this man, and demonstrates once again the humanizing value of a note, even a note inconveniently situated. "The
custom of beginning all *Poems,* with a *Proposition* of the whole
work, and Invocation of some God for his assistance to go
through with it, is solemnly and religiously observed by all
the ancient Poets, that though I could have found out a better way, I should not (I think) have ventured upon it."[3] This is
a fine expression of the tension between custom and innova-
tion that affects a poet at every turn, whether when paying
appropriate dues to the muse or when simply searching for a
word that both rhymes and makes sense.

The first book of *Davideis* has the satisfying ratio of sixteen
pages of notes to twenty-four pages of verse; the three following books have a similar ratio, but we will restrict ourselves to
one or two more samples. Line after line of tightly constructed couplets delight us, each meeting the requirements
of five stressed syllables per line and ending with a welcome
clink-clink of rhyme. Suddenly, Cowley puzzles us with an apparent lapse:

Nor can the glory contain it self in th'endless space.[4]

Cowley anticipates our ear's earnest objections, answering
them with this note: "I am sorry that it is necessary to ad-
monish the most part of Readers, that it is not by negligence
that this verse is so loose, long, and as it were Vast; I would
have observed in divers other places of this Poem, that else will
ask for very careless verses. . . ." Here Cowley provides a list of
other extra-long lines, and then continues, "The thing is, that

---

3. Ibid., p. 66.
4. Ibid., p. 242.

the disposition of words and numbers should be such, as that out of the order and sound of them, the things themselves may be represented. . . ."[5] The reader is thus reassured that Cowley has planned his extra syllables in advance, and that once having written his lines he has—with a discriminating ear—reread them.

This fine annotator's limitations must be mentioned. His splendid notes inform, instruct, and contain entertaining digressions and meticulous scholarship; but they remain the notes of a careful reader, albeit a reader of his own work. The notes do not function *within* the drama of the poem. When, for example, Cowley has *Envy* "crawl" out onto his iambic pentameter stage, all eyes are instantly drawn to her, for ". . . her black locks hung long, / Attir'd with curling *Serpents* . . . at her breast stuck *Vipers* which did prey / Upon her panting heart, . . . sucking black *blood* from thence." Her only slightly overlong speech carries the readers—that is, the audience—along with its vivid depiction of the power of envy and of her "faithful *Snakes,*" which *"Fires"* and "proud *Element* affright."[6] Nearing the conclusion, Envy hisses, "By Me *Cain* Offer'd up his Brothers gore. . . ." A tiny margin note directing us to Genesis 4:8 is a slight distraction at this tense moment—a low whisper, say, from some scholar sitting a row behind. But the reference mark [#16] directing us to the back of the book is a less forgivable intrusion.[7]

The note in and of itself is of interest. Cowley carefully details the limits of our knowledge about the murderous Cain,

---

5. Ibid., p. 66.
6. Ibid., p. 246.
7. Ibid., p. 247.

and the poetic license that it necessitated. The Bible gives us no clue as to "what manner he slew his *Brother;* And therefore I had the Liberty to chuse that which I thought the most probable; which is, that he knockt him on the head with some great stone. . . ." And the poet insists also: "That this stone was big enough to be the *Monument* or *Tombstone* of *Abel,* is not so *Hyperbolical.* . . ."[8] Whatever the note's inherent interest, however, it fails to push forward the plot, it fails to take its place on the main stage of this drama. The note is a serious distraction: a knowledgeable friend, we will say, who whispers into our ears, or who else simply sits muttering to himself, so overflowing with information is he.

Several decades and a good deal of spying must pass before the note will play an active role in poetry's drama. England's Civil War will have petered out, Charles the First's head and Cromwell's pretensions been disposed of, the era of James the Second and Alexander Pope come into view, and then will come Aphra Behn, who makes the note (and the footnote, at that) a fully functioning actor in a poem.

Aphra Behn is generally thought of as the first female professional writer to produce a substantial body of work in English. Her reputation suffered among her contemporaries because she was unmarried for most of her life and because she had a room of her own. Disdain was furthered by a murky past, and by her profusion of names. She was variously referred to as Affara, Ann, Anne, or Aphra, the last the name the patron saint of prostitutes; she herself seems to have preferred Astrea, the "ambivalent virginal and fecund goddess of justice."[9] This confusion may have been deliberate on her

---

8. Ibid., p. 270.

9. Janet Todd, ed., *The Works of Aphra Behn* (Columbus: Ohio State University Press, 1992), p. ix.

part, for like her contemporary Abraham Cowley, she was a
royalist spy, in her case sent to Antwerp to contact a prospec-
tive double agent.[10]

That she was directly influenced by Abraham Cowley's verse
or annotation isn't certain; she did, though, translate some of
his *Sylva* from the Latin into English, and would have recognized the effectiveness and limitations of the many margin
notes and footnotes found in that work.* What *is* certain is
that in time she did him one better with her own footnotes in
A Letter to a Brother of the Pen in Tribulation. In this poem the
footnote is more than a helpful (if distracting) member of the
audience; it takes on a role analogous to the magician's
stooge, apparently one of us, when in fact a partner in the creation of an illusion—a double agent of the theater.

> *A Letter* gets to its point quickly but subtly:
> Poor *Damon!* Art thou caught? Is't ev'n so?
> Art thou become a **Tabernacler* too?[11] [The asterisk is Behn's.]

The urgency of three short sentences and the compact "Is't
ev'n" can be expected from a practiced pro; the asterisk,
though, is sublime. A tabernacle has deeply religious conno-
tations; the asterisk (little star) we might expect to direct us
toward the heavens. But no, of course not. Rather than upward, this star leads us to the bottom of the page, where we
find "[*]So he called a Sweating-Tub."[12] This tabernacler isn't

---

10. Ibid., p. xvii.

* Her translation does not include those notes either because her publisher was frightened by the added expense or because her Latin was not
up to it. John Dryden questioned her Latin skills. See Janet Todd, ed., *The
Works of Aphra Behn* (Columbus: Ohio State University Press, 1992), p. 443.

11. Ibid., p. 72.

12. Ibid.

at prayers at all; he is "taking the cure" for pox.* Two lines later, Behn ensures that even the most ordinary reader will not mistake this as a religious offering:

> This holy [a] time I little thought thy sin
> Deserv'd a *Tub* to do its Pennance in.[13]

The perhaps unnecessary footnote is "[a] Lent."[14] No one has yet given a persuasive reason why Behn employs [a] instead of the dagger or double asterisk as modern readers would expect; she may have wished to recognize the lesser importance of this note. However, subsequent notes, though undoubtedly of importance, continue to use the lowercase letter; most likely Behn, like Homer, occasionally nodded. Those subsequent notes make the crucial point that she has a professional and not simply a personal relationship with her "Brother of the Pen." To her complaint that the brother is fooling around ". . . Just when the Wits had greatest [b] need of you. . . ." is attached the note "[b] I wanted a Prologue to a Play" followed up by a second note "[c] He [the brother] pretended to Retire to Write."[15] His betrayal was of the word, not

---

* Anyone may be tempted to extend the analysis of this ingenious "reversal of the hero's fortune." The tabernacle is often thought of as the "temporary abode of the soul," a notion that Behn's two-directional asterisk makes nicely ambiguous. The tabernacle was crucial during the Israelites' years of wandering; Behn's displeasure that the "brother" for whom she obviously has affection "went wandering" is evident. The attentive reader will notice that this critic has put such perhaps salacious speculations down here rather than in the "body" of the text. For uses of the word *tabernacle* see Stuart Berg Flexnor, editor in chief, *The Random House Dictionary of the English Language*, 2nd ed. (New York: Random House, 1987), p. 1933.

13. Janet Todd, ed., *The Works of Aphra Behn* (Columbus: Ohio State University Press, 1992), p. 72.

14. Ibid.

15. Ibid., p. 73.

the body, and hell hath no fury like a writer scorned—as Pope almost said.

Behn could easily have dispensed with her notes. The verse "Art thou become a *Tabernacler too?" could have become "You must sit in Sweating-Tubs too?" without much damage to rhythm and rhyme. But Behn sets up the reader like a good comedian: "this is a religious poem," she hints. A pause as the reader finds the bottom of the page. Then the footnote, "no this is a poem about pox," is delivered like a punch line. The timing is everything.

Sadly, Aphra Behn died in 1689 at the age of forty-nine without fully developing her annotative skills; left wandering, the footnote fell into the unkind hands of Alexander Pope and his gang of literate layabouts.* Pope seems to have taken an instant dislike to Behn and her poetic experiments. He was a person of strict couplets and pruned bushes and well-tended lawns; she was not. She loved to travel, to sightsee, and to have the chance to spy; he preferred Twickenham and the gossip of close friends. She was attractive; he was not. Long after her death, when she surely offered no competition to him for a patron's notice or the scarce publisher's shilling, Pope included her in his catalog of poetic lapses, *Peri Bathous: or, Martinus Scriblerus, His Treatise of the Art of Sinking in Poetry*. He shoehorns a bit of her expansive *The Golden Age: A Paraphrase on a Translation of French* into the narrow confines of his couplet bias and prods it to stand up and dance. A grove in Eden is the location of her poem. There the flowers twined, and then:

> Exchang'd their sweets, and mix'd with thousand kisses
> As if the willing branches strove
> To beautify and shade the grove

---

* *Layabouts* may strike some as too harsh a term for Pope's coterie. They did some writing certainly, and took long walks, but spent an awful lot of their time lying around Pope's living room gossiping and joking.

Here Pope nudges the reader with his elbow, whispering, "which indeed most branches do."[16] If Behn, indeed, has made a slightly unnecessary observation, one senses from Pope an unnecessary severity. That could be attributed, perhaps, to the extra—and in Pope's eyes untidy—syllable of *kisses* or even, one supposes, to the word *kisses* itself, given Pope's romantic troubles. Confirmation of this comes in a mean-spirited couplet in which Pope takes advantage of his era's prejudice that women found loitering near theaters are "loose." A play of Behn's having had success, Pope hisses (using one of her pen names, Astrea):

> The stage how loosely does Astrea tread
> Who safely puts all characters to bed.[17]

Such versified pettiness would matter little if Pope had not followed up with *The Dunciad Variorum*. We are forced to leave the inventive Behn for the moment to confront Pope's scurrilous and scattershot attack on footnotes disguised as a satire of women poets—and of most of the male poets of the time as well. Commentary on the poem has concentrated on the extravagant conceits of this mock epic. Writers of any stripe find it hard to resist the scene in which publishers, desperate to sign up some of the women writers of popular romances, engage in a contest to see who can urinate the farthest.[18] Publishers, in turn, must find it hard to resist the scene in which Pope brings several writers to the middle of a London bridge. The writers peer down into what is essentially an open sewer in whose

16. Rosemary Cowler, *The Prose Works of Alexander Pope* (Hamden, Conn.: Archon, 1986), p. 219.

17. See George Woodcock, *The English Sappho* (Montreal and New York: Black Rose Books, 1989), p. 102.

18. Alexander Pope, *The Dunciad Variorum With the Prolegomena of Scriblerus* (Princeton, N.J.: Princeton University Press, 1929), pp. 36–8.

"disemboguing streams / Rolls the large tribute of dead dogs to Thamses."[19] A Pope footnote tells everyone that the writers "delight in flinging dirt," at which point they obligingly dive headfirst toward the dogs, and Pope washes his hands of them.[20]

For the attractions of the text, a careful reader finds footnotes are *The Dunciad*'s obvious target. The work, after all, starts with a note. The title itself receives an asterisk. Below, a well-known critic sputters: "It may be well disputed whether this be a right Reading: Ought it not rather be spelled *Dunceiad,* as the Etymology evidently demands: *Dunce* with an *e,* there *Dunceiad* with an *e.* . . ." and continues for another fourteen tiny and intricately punctuated lines, solely about that *e.* Immediately following, the editor strikes a defensive note: "I have a just value for the Letter E, and the same affection for the Name of this Poem, as the forecited Critic for that of his Author . . . ," and so forth.[21] In the succeeding seventy-nine pages 358 lines of pentameter verse are chattered at from below by approximately* 7,000 lines of notes. The centrality of footnotes is further shown as the poem names and defames several of the era's most formida-

---

19. Ibid., p. 43.
20. Ibid., p. 44.
21. Ibid., p. 1.

* The count was achieved in the following manner. A page was found to have 7¼ inches of usable space. Seventy-nine pages provide 572 inches of usable space. Each inch of page space can accommodate four lines of verse; the 358 lines of the poem, therefore, take 89½ inches, which was rounded to 90, leaving 482 inches for the notes. The notes in smaller print and double columns fit sixteen lines into an inch. Four hundred eighty-two inches of page space could house up to 7,712 lines of notes; this has been rounded off to account for the unused space between notes. A precise count would be of interest but seems beyond this present writer's patience.

ble annotators—one in particular, the armed and dangerous Richard Bentley.*

Bentley deserves far more than the paragraph or two we can allot him. Installed as the twentieth master of Trinity College at Cambridge just as the eighteenth century began, he used his scholarship and footnotes to improve the work of Horace, Homer, Milton, and miscellaneous other poets. He exploited his position at Trinity, and Trinity's money, to improve his lifestyle. A new coach for his wife, three new coach houses, a scarlet cloth bed, a damask bed, walnut tables, a granary, a cow house, and a double-vaulted wine cellar appeared shortly after he was installed. Dr. Bentley had the college term shortened at both ends and, presumably to take advantage of the longer summer vacation thus available, he had a country house built for himself with college funds on college land.[22] He had finally overreached himself. In 1734 he received a sentence of deprivation of his position for financial irregularities, as well as for calling one Trinity fellow an ass and a second an old shoe.[23] He was ordered to vacate the master's house; he did not, of

---

* Commentators have, of course, always paid attention to the use of the footnote in *The Dunciad Variorum* as a satirical weapon employed against certain scholars, writers, and publishers. Peter W. Cosgrove, in 1991, is the first to properly emphasize that Pope was using the footnote against itself. "Pope's real intent may be seen, . . . not as a defense of individual word but as a defense of poetry in general against textual criticism." P. W. Cosgrove, "Undermining the Text: Edward Gibbon, Alexander Pope, and the Anti-Authenticating Footnote in *Annotation and Its Texts*," ed. Stephen A. Barney (New York and Oxford: Oxford University Press, 1991), p. 138. See also Anthony Grafton, *The Footnote: A Curious History* (Cambridge, Mass.: Harvard University Press, 1997), pp. 111–8.

22. R. J. White, *Dr. Bentley: A Study in Academic Scarlet* (London: Eyre & Spottiswoode, 1965), p. 206.

23. Ibid., p. 152.

course. He remained there for eight more years until, still squatting, he died in one of his own fine beds.

Bentley's scholarship also overreached itself. His improvements of the writings of Romans and Greeks, though controversial, were justified by the corruption of the texts brought about by the years of copying and recopying during the centuries before the printing press. His reconstruction of a blind man's *Paradise Lost*, however, was condemned with fervent patriotism—Alexander Pope taking the lead, flag and mock footnotes in hand.* (It did not help Pope's mood that scuttlebutt had Dr. Bentley saying of Pope's translation of Homer, "A pretty poem, Mr. Pope, but you must not call it Homer."[24]) The fourth book of *The Dunciad* was devoted to evicting Bentley from the house of scholarship as if under a writ of satire.

Bentley could not be expected to go easily. A fellow scholar who ran afoul of Bentley received a bullet hole in the wainscot of his study. Bentley, both of whose grandfathers fought in the English Civil War, was thought to be the most likely suspect.[25] No wonder Pope took to carrying pistols and bringing

---

* Bentley, it has to be said, deserved some firm correction, if not Pope's bullying. Milton has Adam and Eve leave Eden with some reluctance. "They hand in hand with wandering steps and slow, / Through Eden took their solitary way." Bentley, a stickler for facts, reminds us that Eve "had professed her Readiness and Alacrity for the journey . . ." and that "there were only the two of them in Eden, and they were not more solitary now than they had been before." But facts are not drama, and Bentley's revision of Milton's verse loses something:

Then hand in hand with social steps their way
Through Eden took, with Heav'ly Comfort Cheer'd.

See R. J. White, *Dr. Bentley: A Study in Academic Scarlet* (London: Eyre & Spottiswoode, 1965), p. 216.

24. R. C. Jebb, *Bentley* (London: Macmillan, 1909), p. 202.

25. White, ibid., p. 22.

his Great Dane with him whenever he went out for a stroll.[26] Nor is it any wonder he lost his nerve for a time, claiming the poem referred to the mild-mannered son of Dr. Bentley and not to Dr. Bentley himself.

The risks that Alexander Pope took, and the maneuvering that he engaged in, suggest the fierce antagonism with which he sought to confront annotators and stamp out annotation. His own annotations were designed to bring the footnote into disrepute. An event much closer to our time, during the 1930s Depression, will help us understand the malicious tactics of Pope. A long-running farce on Broadway contained an effusive panegyric to Harvard. A Yalie took offense. One night he recruited a few dozen Skid Row bums (as they were known then), plied them with liquor, bought them tickets to the show, and gave them very firm instructions. When the praise of Harvard ended, scruffy, foul-smelling men popped up throughout the audience to cheer and to sing Harvard's fight song. The university's endowment has remained strong, but its reputation among the cognoscenti has never fully recovered.

Pope had his footnotes pop up in the same way—shabby, tipsy, and scented with bogus academicism—and to the same effect. The poetic footnote, and particularly the kind of dramatically integrated note that Aphra Behn pioneered, was never fully developed. That Pope had Behn's work particularly in mind, at least when he began *The Dunciad Variorum,* we can argue with some confidence. Pope's first footnote, as we have seen, is an asterisk just like Behn's in "A Letter to a Brother." After that he refuses to use any more reference marks in the text at all, a subtle dig at Behn, who similarly immediately changed her mind and used [a] and [b] for her succeeding

26. Maynard Mack, *Alexander Pope: A Life* (London: W. W. Norton, 1985), p. 489.

footnotes. Pope quite clearly is saying that he can employ the footnote, particularly the ersatz footnote, without interrupting the marvelously interminable flow of his verse; sadly, his tidy mind could not conceive of the dramatic possibilities inherent in the poetic footnote.

Some will find the Pope/Behn connection tenuous and, lacking Pope's self-confidence or temper, this admirer of both poetry and footnotes can only shake his head in bafflement and sorrow. Behn finally now is receiving the recognition as poet and dramatist and novelist and spy that she deserves; she should also add to her laurels as the pioneer of annotation.

In scholarly circles the footnote flourished despite Pope's attack; it survived even in poetry—though there Pope's unfortunate influence was much more widespread—but never with the élan that Behn had endowed it. In the end its use in the arts in general became suspect everywhere. In France the literary footnote's reputation sank so low that by the 1770s footnotes could be used by pornographers for mere titillation.[27] A sad ending after such a bright beginning.

---

27. Anthony Grafton, *The Footnote: A Curious History* (Cambridge: Harvard University Press, 1997), p. III.

4

The Years of Discipline

As the eighteenth century approached, the footnote became the young hero of a picaresque novel. Like the goodhearted Tom Jones,* he found himself scrambling from one hair-raising and unsavory adventure to another; like Barry Lyndon, he moved through every stratum of society and across national borders; like Simplicissimus, he found some respectable occupations and some shady ones; and, as is the case with all such heroes, he was from time to time saved from idleness and disgrace by the kind, firm, and unexpected ministrations of a miscellanea of tutors.

For the footnote, those tutors were most importantly the exuberant Frenchman Pierre Bayle; the hearty, rhetorical Englishman Edward Gibbon; and the meticulous, somewhat dull German Leopold von Ranke. All of them, with very different methods, took the footnote into their homes, gave him lessons—sternly or gently—and sent him on his way better

---

* Poor Tom Jones has had questions raised about his picaresque status—he seems always to have his status questioned. Common sense, however, should convince us that a hero who travels as much as Tom, and who suffers as many pratfalls as Tom, is picaresque. For a contrary view and fuller discussion of this, see Stuart Miller, *The Picaresque Novel* (Cleveland and London: The Press of Case Western Reserve University, 1967), pp. 131–5.

equipped to make a living and (metaphorically) a sensible marriage. That the footnote sat still long enough to be usefully instructed by such contradictory masters proves his resilience, his determination to make his mark on the world, however unprepossessing his origins.

From where we stand now, from this distance of centuries, the formidable writings of Bayle, Gibbon, and Ranke stand out clearly against the cultural horizon of Europe's landscape, cluttered though it is with the works of the great, the near-great, and the merely mediocre. But at the time the footnote was lucky to find them, and because of them also find temporary housing and a lasting education. Bayle's great sixteenth-century *Dictionnaire Historique et Critique* is an immense, rambling farmhouse through which the loud Bayle pulled the footnote by the elbow, scattering chickens and attracting pigs, causing cows to lift their heads from their grazing, and sending horses trotting off nervously to the far end of the pasture. Gibbon's *The History of the Decline and Fall of the Roman Empire* makes a stately and logical impression, the estate of someone used to speaking before Parliament and bowing before kings. There the footnote learned to keep his head up during many rotund after-dinner speeches, and learned to keep his eyes open and to catch the quick, quirkish asides, the sly, personal attacks, the bits of arcane knowledge, the fragments of wisdom. Ranke's scholarly tomes present themselves as a row of immaculate town houses of sensible size, compatible with each other though with subtle distinctions sufficient to keep a passerby's interest. Inside, the footnote was to find only straight-backed chairs to sit on, plain food to eat, and a whiff of schoolmaster's chalk accompanying the scent of roses. In these three oddly different establishments the character of the footnote was shaped, his future determined. To understand the history of the footnote is to understand those three educators.

Pierre Bayle was a charming if cantankerous man cursed to live in an interesting time. Son of a Protestant pastor in Catholic France during the years when the Church tightened the bonds of intolerance about alternative faiths with excruciating meticulousness, he was a fierce pamphleteer in the War between the Sects. Eventually he fled to Holland as to a bolt-hole. (The Revocation of the Edict of Nantes, an act that sealed the fate of the Protestants in France, was issued in 1685 when Bayle was thirty-eight.) From there he continued to infuriate French authorities by publishing works that tied scholarship to sarcasm in an enchanting, dangerous style. Even his enemies occasionally laughed out loud: not something the men who felt responsible for everyone's salvation could accept.

And they didn't; they went after him with a vengeance.

An unwary Bayle gave them their chance. His writings were published without his name attached to them, anonymity providing some protection for himself and his family. But then he put out an advertisement that let his name be known. Why? He felt obliged, he is reported to have said, to let the public know that "the Magistrates of Rotterdam honour the Muses with protection, and that this work was composed by one of the professors whom they had settled in their *New Illustrious School*."[1] His explanation is inadequate. Honoring the men who gave him sanctuary—and a job—may have been

---

1. Peter [sic] Bayle, *The Dictionary, Historical and Critical* (London: printed for J. J. and P. Knapton; D. Midwinter; J. Brotherton; A. Bettesworth, C. Hitch . . . [and 25 others], 1734–1738), 2nd ed., p. xxiii. The original French edition was published in 1696, but this edition is more convenient for the general reader. *F*'s in the text have been replaced by *S*'s.

part of the motive behind the advertisement, but surely an author's pride at gaining an international audience must have been a subsidiary motive. He was, after all, a pastor's son who had grown up on a farm, with plenty of books to read but also with plenty of messy chores to do. His family had been poor enough so only one child at a time could be sent to secondary school; Pierre had had to wait while the eldest son, Jacob, preceded him before getting his own chance. And the academy he went to did not, of course, have the prestige of the Catholic universities from which Protestants were excluded. Bayle was a self-made man and proud of it; his pride led to carelessness.

The French authorities, now knowing for certain the identity of the troublemaker, still were unable to get at Pierre Bayle himself, so they scooped up his quiet brother Jacob, still in France, and stuck him in prison. Five months of bad food in a damp cell and daily visits from an importuning Jesuit priest asking him to recant were enough to kill him. Terrible guilt assailed Pierre Bayle—and toughened him. He lost his faith in a divine providence; whether he kept his faith in God is a matter of dispute. (Many early writers dismissed him as a cynic and nonbeliever; more recent writers accept his constant claim to believe in a God, though a God many would not recognize.) The source of evil in a universe created by a beneficent God became a question that bedeviled him. In the end, like many more recent theologians, the best he could do, as a later writer puts it, is to "declare a moratorium on the use of human reasoning. When, as we must, we call God holy, just and good, we should realize that these terms cannot have their purely human sense."[2]

---

2. Elisabeth Labrousse, *Bayle* (Oxford and New York: Oxford University Press, 1983), p. 63. Labrousse is the source of Bayle's life unless otherwise specified.

We must keep in mind Bayle's desolation, his guilt and anger at what intolerance and his own pride wrought when we turn to his magnificent dictionary, a work in which the full splendor of footnotes is first demonstrated. Bayle thought of the dictionary originally as a compilation of other writers' errors, a reference work in which one could find out everything that had been misstated about Aristotle, Rome, the expulsion of Adam and Eve from Eden, or any of the other figures, places, and events that stocked the mind of a well-educated seventeenth-century reader. He compared the task he set for himself to the cutting off of the Hydra heads or the cleaning of the Augean stables.[3] It was the perfect image for someone convinced that intolerance bred of ignorance has fouled the world—and convinced that he has a brother's death from intolerance on his conscience.

Cooler heads prevailed, and persuaded Bayle that even the most dedicated scholar did not want in his library multiple volumes devoted to other writers' errors, any more than a mathematician would want a book of invalid equations or a farmer sacks of bad seed. Bayle finally agreed to provide the facts as he found them in a conventional presentation of alphabetized entries. But then, in what must have been one of those *eureka* moments of inventive genius, Bayle realized that he could have it both ways. The text could provide the true accounts, but errors and the chastisement of those errors could

3. Pierre Bayle, "Projet d'un Dictionaire critique," in *Projet et fragments d'un Dictionaire critique* (Rotterdam, 1692; repr. Geneva, 1970), sig. *2 verso. Quoted in Anthony Grafton, *The Footnote: A Curious History* (Cambridge, Mass.: Harvard University Press, 1997), p. 193. Grafton gives an account of Bayle's achievement that manages to be both succinct and thoughtful. His emphasis, however, is on the intellectual development of the footnote, an account that fails, in my eyes, to catch the full expansiveness of Bayle, or the humanity of Bayle's footnote.

be put into long, digressive, unlimited footnotes. Footnotes
that seem to breed among themselves and multiply like the
proverbial rabbit, or split apart and split apart again like the
indomitable amoeba. Footnotes that take up more space than
the text and have as least as much interest. Footnotes that
swish like swords ensuring the Hydra's heads of error rattle to
the bottom of the page and collect there, the detritus of ignorance. Footnotes that frequently chastise, as Bayle exercises his
judgmental side.

The five volumes of *The Dictionary, Historical and Critical,* in
the edition that now occupies my desk, weigh in at forty
pounds. Opened, a volume spreads out to an ample fourteen
by twenty inches.* Open its last volume and you find just
over 9 of its 1,015 pages allocated to the great Roman poet
Virgil. His nine pages have forty-four lines of text and 1,144
footnotes of commentary. One hundred and nine additional
margin notes refer us to Bayle's sources or, in a rare case or
two, provide additional information. Commentary can delve
into deeply personal biography: for example, a refutation of
the charge that Virgil was "inclined to unnatural sin."[4] A
note can begin as a correction of a critic's grammar: "[Mr.
Moréri's] manner of placing his words . . . ,"[5] then lead us off
to a margin note for a grammar lesson: "Logic teaches us
that in all compounded and copulative propositions, all the
attributes sought to agree. . . ."—a note that ends by referring

---

* For the sake of comparison: A two-volume edition of the nineteenth-
century heavyweight *War and Peace* weighs three and a half pounds; a
Remembrance of Things Past edition is four pounds. The latter, opened, is a
perfectly adequate eight by twelve inches.

4. Peter *[sic]* Bayle, *The Dictionary, Historical and Critical* (London: printed
for J. J. and P. Knapton; D. Midwinter; J. Brotherton; A. Bettesworth, C.
Hitch . . . [and 25 others], 1734–1738), 2nd ed., vol. 5, p. 484, note [A].

5. Ibid., p. 491, note [L].

us to the *"Art of Thinking, Part. Ii, ch. ix. . . ."*[6] should we wish further instruction.

What Bayle chooses to include in his dictionary can be pleasantly idiosyncratic, and reflects his own life in a way that is charming, even touching. The River Auriege is one of those entries. The Auriege has no great claim on a historian's time. Though Bayle assures us it is "full of Fish and also very good to drink,"[7] that surely could have been said of any number of French backwaters that were left to splash and gurgle unreported upon by Bayle. But the Auriege entry in the dictionary hits a Wordsworthian note of reminiscence and homage. Once when young, Bayle studied so fervently that he made himself sick, and was sent to a country house "situate *[sic]* on the banks of the Auriege."[8] Twenty years later he remembers the fish and the refreshing water and his slow recovery, and he gives thanks to the Auriege. We appreciate this human touch but, as Bayle must have counted on, seek an intellectual justification for our time wandering along the river in footnotes. At the bottom of the page, seventeen inches of commentary sort out the proper name for the river, whether Auriege or Ariege. The sorting out takes us over to the martyrdom of "St. Antonim *[sic]*" and requires us to watch the saint's body being placed on a raft and floated down the river. We are also presented with a critique of a map whose "Proper names" are so "disfigured, that we ought to suppose them to be faults of the engraver."[9] The critique in turn provides an opportunity for Bayle to grab us firmly by the arm and argue: "I know

6. Ibid., note [74].

7. Peter *[sic]* Bayle, *The Dictionary, Historical and Critical* (London: printed for J. J. and P. Knapton; D. Midwinter; J. Brotherton; A. Bettesworth, C. Hitch . . . [and 25 others], 1734–1738), 2nd ed., vol. 1, p. 579.

8. Ibid., p. iii.

9. Ibid., p. 579, note [A].

many Authors make a jest of a Writer who takes them up for Errors of this Nature, and pretend to be above those Trifles: But they are vain Pretenders who want a Fair Mask to cover either their Ignorance or their Idleness, or their ill Taste, or their Incorrectness."[10] This last remark makes the twist and turns of Bayle's mind transparent. The Pretenders' possible failings are hammered home as if they were four nails needed to hold up a particularly ugly poster: *bang*, Ignorance, *bang*, *bang*, Idleness, ill Taste, or, if none of those failings then simply flat out, *bang*, Incorrectness. We follow the trail of his thought wherever it leads, from text to footnote to margin note, to text, to another footnote. The bumps and curves of the scholarly mind are mapped for us in a way no simple text lying inert on the page can do.

The footnote does not exhaust our interest in the Auriege nor, indeed, does a second one that explores the river's various tributaries, the Lers, the Arget, the Leze, and so forth. And since a sonneteer has made verse out of his love for the river, Bayle, determined to do homage, finds room for the complacent rhymes. "Auriege, thou noble River," it begins in the translated version, "known to Fame / for thy bright waters, and thy golden name . . . ,"[11] and known now because of Bayle's golden memories.

The *Dictionnaire historique et critique* was an immediate and overwhelming success. An educated person in the eighteenth century was more likely to have Bayle's work in his library than to have something by Locke or Voltaire or Newton or Rousseau. "In fact it was to become the philosophical block-

---

10. Ibid.
11. Ibid., p. 579, note [C].

buster of all time."[12] One is tempted to ascribe the dictionary's popularity simply to the insatiable desire of scholars of that era for reliable facts and to their gratitude for the inspiration someone else's work could provide them. Voltaire (not someone who needed any other person's inspiration, of course) had a love/hate relationship with the dictionary and with Bayle. He was dismayed by Bayle's carelessness, his failure to "chastise" or to correct his prose.[13] The great eighteenth-century art historian J. J. Winckelmann was so smitten by the dictionary that he copied out "1300 pages of articles . . . in a minute hand."[14] Testimony from other scholars would be easy to supply.

It is equally tempting—perhaps even more tempting—to attribute Bayle's success to the amount of controversial, often salacious material that found its way into the dictionary and

12. Thomas M. Lennon, *Reading Bayle* (Toronto, Buffalo, and London: University of Toronto Press, 1999), p. 7. Lennon mentions "[s]helf counts of private libraries" but does not supply a reference. Though Lennon is surely correct about the book's popularity, the lack of footnote citation is unfortunate. As Lennon himself notes, Bayle's dictionary is no longer a staple of public, let alone private, libraries. Skeptical readers may take it on faith that Bayle outsold Locke or Rousseau. But Plato? For this, rigorous proof surely is needed. Plato, incidentally, is not to be found in Bayle's dictionary; Bayle apparently was satisfied with the entry in Louis Moréri's earlier dictionary—a rare agreement between the two. Moréri was a favorite target of Bayle's footnotes. See Elisabeth Labrousse, *Bayle* (Oxford and New York: Oxford University Press, 1983), p. 41. As the reader undoubtedly has noticed, Bayle's habit of digression is as easily caught as the Asian flu.

13. Quoted in H. T. Mason, *Pierre Bayle and Voltaire* (London: Oxford University Press, 1963), p. 10: Bayle "n'a jamais châtié son style. . . ."

14. A. Tibal, *Inventaire des manuscrits de Winckelmann déposés à la Bibliothèque Nationale* (Paris, 1911), p. 12. Quoted in Anthony Grafton, *The Footnote: A Curious History* (Cambridge, Mass.: Harvard University Press, 1997), p. 195. Grafton is also the source of many of the leads to works on Bayle that I have used without directly crediting him.

into his footnotes in particular. The French New Wave cinema of the 1950s provides a useful analogy. Much criticism of those films engages in a highly rarefied intellectual analysis of Goddard's distancing devices, for example, or of Truffaut's homage to Hitchcock. But one aging American critic recently admitted that his initial, youthful interest in the New Wave (and for that matter the interest of many of his colleagues) could be attributed to the films' homage to nudity.

In any case, a reader expects an article on Abel to raise sensitive theological issues, but most readers will be taken aback to find Bayle assuring them (in the text) that he will "not venture into any Conjectures upon the Question, Whether [Abel] died a *Virgin*."[15] And no reader, even if not an adolescent film buff, will pass by the footnote inserted at that place—no more than a viewer of Goddard's *Contempt* would go out for popcorn as Brigitte Bardot appears languid and naked on the screen.* The footnote [D] uses up a modest three inches of column to talk about just what the reader has been assured Bayle will avoid; the footnote allows him to have his dignity and his audience-grabber too.[16]

<hr>

15. Peter *[sic]* Bayle, *The Dictionary, Historical and Critical* (London: printed for J. J. and P. Knapton; D. Midwinter; J. Brotherton; A. Bettesworth, C. Hitch . . . [and 25 others], 1734–1738), 2nd ed., vol. 1, p. 23.

* The story of Bardot's disrobing is part of moviemaking lore. Apparently Goddard's financial backers insisted on it; they undoubtedly had in mind the American market of young, intellectual males.

16. Peter *[sic]* Bayle, *The Dictionary, Historical and Critical* (London: printed for J. J. and P. Knapton; D. Midwinter; J. Brotherton; A. Bettesworth, C. Hitch . . . [and 25 others], 1734–1738), 2nd ed., vol. 1, p. 23, note [D]. The note begins: "Some Fathers of the Church have maintained the Affirmative [18]; and the Heretics, taken notice of below, who took their names from *Abel* are of the same opinion; but those who believe, that *Abel* lived an hundred and twenty nine Years, think it improbable he should die a *Batchelor [sic]*."

A reader for whom footnote [D] has proved attractive and who has any knowledge of medieval theologians will certainly immediately move on to the next article, the one on Abelard. Peter Abelard's life is an opera with a wonderfully rich, singing,* intellectual content and the frisson of his doomed love for Heloise. Who can resist a peek at Bayle's almost cinematic treatment of a monk whose careful reasoning got his "On the Divine Unity and Trinity" torched by an ecclesiastical council and whose unrestrained passion for a woman got him castrated by an angry uncle?

But Bayle is a subtle artist. In effect, he turns the camera away during the most gruesome scene; a simple sentence, a few phrases, is sufficient to "unman" Abelard. With the sure, instinctive judgment of a master, Bayle prefers to dwell on the complex motives that pushed Abelard toward his grim fate rather than the gore. The text, like a camera's long shot, quickly establishes the scene: footnote [G], which is immediately inserted, is like an intense, hovering close-up of a deeply troubled face, freezing time, requiring us to meditate on the character and destiny of Abelard: "Vanity was our Hero's distinguishing Foible," the footnote like a voice-over tells us, "However, being an handsome young Fellow, and in the Flower of his age; and having a knack at Poetry, a great Reputation, and Money in his Pocket; it is not so strange that he Flattered himself with a kind Reception, whenever he should make his Addresses. . . ."[17] The

---

* "Indeed, [Abelard] communicates a singing quality to topics ordinarily unmelodious. Few other Scholastics remain as readable and alive": Paul Edwards, editor in chief, *The Encyclopedia of Philosophy* (New York and London: Macmillan and The Free Press, Collier Macmillan Publishers, 1967), vol. 1, p. 6.

17. Peter *[sic]* Bayle, *The Dictionary, Historical and Critical* (London: printed for J. J. and P. Knapton; D. Midwinter; J. Brotherton; A. Bettesworth, C. Hitch . . . [and 25 others], 1734–1738), 2nd ed., vol. 1, p. 27, note [G].

long shot is held, and the voice-over continues, "[Abelard] touched the heart of Eloise *[sic],* and fired her so by his charming Pen, and enchanting Voice that the poor Lady could never overcome her Passion."[18] Now a quick shot of Heloise's young face. (Bayle and his camera send us from footnote [H] of the Abelard article to footnote "[F] under [Heloise's] Article. . . .")[19] An interior voice, trembling with passion, tells us: ". . . his love verses were so pretty, and his songs so agreeable, both as to the words and airs, that every body[*] was charmed with them . . . ; they were as much taken with his person, and loved him passionately. . . ."[20] Heloise's voice fades; a new analytic voice begins: "As [Heloise] loved Abelard even to distraction, she fancied no women could look upon him, but must fall into the same passion": a nice, complicating bit of irony that keeps this love story from being simply another Hollywood tear-jerker.

The complications are not finished. Thanks to the versatility of Bayle's footnotes, a darker theme emerges. We are taken back to Abelard, where the text like a short tracking shot observes him "amusing himself in toying and kissing her,"[21] then cuts quickly to footnote [H]. "The better to disguise his Design from the Uncle, he pretended sometimes to make use of the Liberty given him of correcting *Eliosa.* He tells us that Love, not the anger of a Teacher, prompted him from time to time to whip his Pupil; but that the Lashes he gave her, were

18. Ibid.

19. Ibid.

[*] Contemporary writers might well envy the seventeenth century's orthographic independence; to separate *everybody* into *every body* in this context supplies a sensuous reverberation that has to be appreciated by the most intellectualized reader (or film critic).

20. Ibid., vol. 3, p. 381, note [F].

21. Ibid., vol. 1, p. 27.

the softest in the World."[22] A brilliant stroke is this: the era's subjugation of women revealed, the subtle self-deceits of Abelard sully his character, and the uncle's unmanning violence foreshadowed, perhaps even inadvertently mocked, by a much too cocky Abelard.

"Bayle's footnotes buzz with the salacious twaddle of the Republic of Letters," it has been said, "with every pornographic interpretation of a biblical passage and every sexual anecdote about a philosopher or a scholar."[23] A certain amount of truth obtains, though one hopes it is not unduly cynical to assume that the scholar making the remark is exaggerating a bit in defending the honor of his profession. The anecdotes, if salacious, are usually true and often germane, as in the case with Abelard and Heloise.

The scholar goes on to offer an example, one that turns out to be more problematic than persuasive. "We owe to [Bayle] the preservation of Caspar Scioppius' description of the sparrow he watched from his student lodgings at Ingolstadt," he writes, "having intercourse twenty times and then dying—as well as Scioppius' reflection, 'O unfair lot. Is this to be granted to sparrows and denied to men?'"[24] Salacious, well, yes, perhaps. But yet do we not welcome something so teasingly funny, something so remindful of our own youthfully lustful

---

22. Ibid., note [H].

23. Anthony Grafton, *The Footnote: A Curious History* (Cambridge, Mass.: Harvard University Press, 1997), p. 197. Grafton could also with justice be called a philosopher, as much of his writing drifts—intelligently and provocatively—into the domain of philosophy.

24. Ibid. But Scioppius's account of his youthful run-in with the sparrow is first in Latin and only later translated by Bayle, which surely limited his audience even in the sixteenth century more effectively that an R rating in the twenty-first.

thoughts, something that makes the serious, bookish Scioppius a human we recognize, that summarizes and dramatizes the urgent desires of men and women in a single Latin cry of frustration?

Even this appealing defense does Bayle an injustice. The story of Scioppius and the sparrow is part of Bayle's well-planned intellectual trap. The note [B] stretches along twenty-nine inches of columns across two pages: a substantial footnote though by no means a particularly long one by Bayle's standard of industry and thoroughness.[25] The note does not stand out; it does not call attention to itself. In fact, the reticent text of the Scioppius article hides its connection to the sparrow story with a confusion of reference marks: ". . . [Scioppius] returned to Altdorf, and published some books of Criticism which made him very proud: he could not see without vanity, his great youth joined to a distinguished merit in print [B]. It is said that one of the early productions of his pen, was commentary upon the Priapeia, which drew a great many reproaches upon him, especially, because therein he envied the condition of sparrows [b]. He made a journey into Italy, and after he had been some time at Verona, he returned into Germany, from whence he went again into Italy. . . ."[26] The reference mark [B] quite deliberately keeps aloof from even the elliptic mention of the sparrow that follows in the text; indeed, the reader who drops down to the note must make his way along a meandering path of small print for some eleven inches before the first mention of the sparrow occurs, and then another couple of

25. Peter [sic] Bayle, The Dictionary, Historical and Critical (London: printed for J. J. and P. Knapton; D. Midwinter; J. Brotherton; A. Bettesworth, C. Hitch . . . [and 25 others], 1734–1738), 2nd ed., vol. 5, pp. 90–1.
  26. Ibid.

inches over rocky and bramble-infested Latin before the translation of the sparrow story appears. One has to wonder whether Bayle didn't sometimes mimic in his prose some of his strolls along the Auriege: a tiresome, erratic walk to a sudden view of rapids and blue sky.

The reader who starts at the [B] pushes through a thickly detailed discussion of the early works of Scioppius and of their reception; he can have no idea of where he will end up. The sly, little [b] cozying up to the uninformative mention of the sparrows is altogether a different matter. It takes us to a margin note: "[b] See the remark [B]."[27] It invests the sparrow with independent significance, but an elusive, tantalizing significance as if from a scholar's unconscious that ordinarily is repressed by social codes and work habits. The reader who goes from [b] to [B] ends up on the same path but now with a nagging question that hurries him forward: Just what is this about? The sexuality of the young Scioppius requires attention, any fair-minded reader would agree; but Bayle has found a way to distance the theme so that far from being salacious (or arousing), it is exhaustive. One is put in mind again of the 1950s French New Wave; yes, in those films there was sufficient "toying and kissing" (to use Bayle's phrase) to supply material for the come-ons of ads and posters; and, yes, the revelations of breasts and behinds put to shame Hollywood's timid and tepid sex; but most of what happened in front of you as you sat in the darkened theater was talk, long, thorough, analytic, often informative, sometimes entertaining, rarely erotic talk. Talk and subtitles. So too with Bayle. Footnotes upon footnotes, like the abrupt montages of

---

27. Ibid., p. 90.

Goddard or the charming voice-overs and discreet camera angles of Truffaut, allow sex to enter academia without becoming salacious—the apple shines in Eden without the wriggling snake.

The subtle permutations wrought on the footnote by Bayle are nowhere better demonstrated, in fact, than in his treatment of Adam and Eve. Though some have questioned Bayle's adherence to Christian theology, he seems to accept the Gospel's account of the first man and first woman without skepticism, and with a sincerity that is palpable. The text is lyrical. "His Body having been formed by the Dust of the Earth [A], God breathed into his Nostrils the Breath of Life; that is to say, he animated him, and made him that Compound Creature, which we call *Man,* comprehending an Organized Body, and a Rational Soul."[28] The phrases sweep forward from that most simple of substances, dust, toward its destiny and, with a chorus of capital letters and italics, turns it into Compound Creature, *Man,* Organized Body, Rational Soul. When Eve joins Adam and they wake to each other's presence, Bayle, contrary to what some might expect, does not even hint at something salacious; and further, when the apple is eaten and they "perceived that they were naked," Bayle immediately has them cover themselves with "Aprons" made from "Fig-leaves."[29] If there remained any chance of an inappropriate response to this delicate passage, the footnote [C] disarms us. "The Scripture says, that *their Eyes were opened.* This Expression made some People believe that *Adam* and *Eve* were *blind,* till *[sic]* they had transgress'd the Commandment

---

28. Ibid., vol. I, p. 101.
29. Ibid.

of God."[30] What follows is a completely academic exposure of this foolish interpretation, a discussion that both diverts attention away from the fact of nakedness *and* reminds us of the lengths to which puritanical exegesis must go lest nakedness in God's place be equated with smut.

Something much more interesting is going on with the article on Adam. The reader soon notices that this central character of the religious drama receives little space: only a bit over four pages, whereas the six pages immediately following are devoted to a motley collection of lesser Adams: a near-contemporary of Bayle, an Adam (no first name) who was made the archdeacon of the Patriarchal Chamber, a John Adam, a Jesuit preacher embroiled in many arcane theological disputes, a Melchior Adam about whom Bayle slyly says, "The indefatigable Care he took to collect, frame, and publish, the Lives of a great number of learned Persons, deserves, that somebody should do him the like Office . . . ,"[31] and, finally, an Adam (again, no first name), "a Joyner of *Nevers,* and a French Poet . . . ,"[32] from which entry we are immediately

---

30. Ibid., note [C].

31. Ibid., p. 110. Bayle probably was not genuinely worried about his own inclusion in later biographical dictionaries; more likely he simply could not pass up a chance for another swipe at Mr. Moréri, his competitor and *bête noir.* Moréri, as Bayle makes sure to point out, does not have an entry in his dictionary for the "indefatigable" Adam.

32. Ibid. The article on Billaut dismisses him with a few brief paragraphs; he "became a pretty good *French* poet" on whom critics "did not lavish praise" and who "did not grow rich by the Poet's Trade" (ibid., vol. 2, p. 9). Poets were a dime a dozen during the seventeenth century—literally. Only some ulterior motive can account for his gaining entry into Bayle's dictionary. That Bayle wanted to surround the first Adam with lesser lights would explain the entry.

sent to another entry under Billaut (this Adam's real name) for a fuller biography.

The list of lesser Adams subtly diminishes the stature of the first man. That this was deliberate on Bayle's part is confirmed by the initial, teasing footnote that quickly interrupts the respectful and dignified text of the first Adam. The note [A] is cloaked in the robes of scholarship, but its intent is to disrobe religious certainty. "If we may believe Father Garaffe [1]," it begins, introducing immediately a fine skeptical tone, *"Photius* reports, the *Egyptian* Tradition, *That Wisdom laid an Egg in the Terrestrial Paradise, out of which came our first Parents like a couple of Chickens."* The first man from dust? The first woman from the man's rib? Or both from an egg? Without directly challenging the Christian tradition, Bayle makes us suspicious of any account of our beginnings, though he is not. Bayle then charges Father Garaffe, "that Jesuit," with "a licentious Paraphrase" of Photius, with having mistaken an Egyptian sailor's name, Oe, with *oon,* the word for "egg." "Many Enquiries might be made about this Egg . . . ,"[33] he claims, and for more stories on the egg he sends us scurrying to his article on Arimanius. There he travels from Egypt to Greece where "[s]ome of the ancients said, that a Dove, brooding on an Egg produced Venus. . . ."[34] And so the wit of Bayle and the flexibility of his footnotes bring the Holy Ghost together with the goddess whom Botticelli made famous as a lithe nude with long hair and ambiguous gaze surfing to shore on a shell. And Bayle does it in the name of responsible scholarship and or-

---

33. Ibid., p. 101, note [A].
34. Ibid., p. 444, note [A].

thodox theology. We would instinctively cheer this virtuoso performance did not the shadow of a dead brother and Bayle's terrible guilt inhibit us; in the end, we must admit, the quick-witted Bayle is nothing if not darkly serious.

Bayle is the Mozart of the footnote. He first recognized the full potential of the form and explored it as deftly and exhaustively as Mozart explored the piano sonata, the string quintet, and, most important, the opera. Bayle opened its riches like a mother lode to the miners and toilers who came after him. What in lesser hands could be simply interruptions and diversions became in Bayle's part of the drama of his prose. To begin with the sober account of Adam in the upper world of the text and then drop down to the netherworld of footnotes is to be alerted that some great change is taking place. To pick one's way through the brier patch of Jesuit and Egyptian scholarship and then to be sent sailing lightly off to the Arimanius article increases the suspense, the excitement. To then arrive at a conjunction of Venus and the Holy Ghost, a conjunction of two reverberating cultures, is to arrive at a climax not unlike the end of *The Magic Flute,* when music and character and plot at last make sense.

As a picaresque hero, the footnote was fortunate to have Bayle for its first important tutor; to learn how to be dramatic, even histrionic, is not a laughable lesson. Something deeper goes on in the *Dictionary, Historical and Critical,* however, which best can be discovered by extending our analogy. The picaresque hero's personality is protean; he can be anything. Over the course of his life, his characteristics are "a servant, an altar boy, a beggar's boy, a constable's man, a water-seller, a wine seller, a town crier. . . ."[35] And also a blind man, a mouse, and a

---

35. Stuart Miller, *The Picaresque Novel* (Cleveland and London: The Press of Case Western Reserve University, 1967), p. 70.

snake! Another is "a mariner, a miller, a baker, a scout, a crosse-biter [an upright man], a cheater, a cozener, a fox. . . ."[36] The picaresque hero is the embodiment of a primitive Id—not the one Freud found in his sophisticated, Vienna version of the un-conscious, with its Ego and Super Ego that internalize law and order, but a pre-Freudian Id. Yes, this is an Id that always re-quires an external control, a hierarchy of class and status, a constabulary, draconian courts, punishment made visible by the feet and arms sticking out of stocks, the scars from whips and branding irons, the necks dangling from ropes.

The seventeenth century remains the perfect place for such a hero, a world always on the brink of chaos, where our foot-note, trained by Bayle, becomes a survivor in a dark, swirling, sometimes upside-down, sometimes inside-out story. Bayle's footnotes are emotional, dramatic, protean characters that put to shame the pallid caricatures to which later scholars sometimes reduced them.

Their next important tutor, Edward Gibbon, did not greet them at the door with a hearty embrace and lead them into the dining room for a meal of roast beef and port. Though Gibbon inherited property, occasionally played the role of country squire, and was afflicted by gout, probably from an overabundance of wine and kidney pie, he was not the horse-riding, hale, red-faced English gentleman Thackeray and a score of other gossips might have led us to expect. No, he was a short, dumpy, indoor man. "I never handled a gun," he con-fessed, "I seldom mounted a horse, and my walks were soon terminated by some shady bench of philosophic contempla-tion."[37] A man who never in his life purchased a fowling piece

---

36. Ibid., p. 71.

37. John Murray, ed., *The Autobiographies of Edward Gibbon* (London: John Murray, 1896), p. 247. Quoted in Patricia B. Craddock, *Young Edward*

but who once brought home 150 writing pens, "100 of them large,"[38] would not fit the stereotype even had he stayed in England instead of running off to France or Switzerland at every excuse. As he grew older, "his tailor's bills constantly include[d] charges for remaking and enlarging garments."[39] A certain Madame du Deffand, a blind aristocrat in the habit of acquiring familiarity with a new acquaintance by stroking the face with her fingers, did so to Gibbon. She was not pleased. The face, "obscured by fat," convinced her that a witless joke had been played on her and "the behind of a naked baby" had been presented to her.[40]

In the beginning Gibbon did not fight for footnotes; he let his publisher stick the commentary and references into the back of the book. Apparently it was David Hume, the skeptical philosopher, who drew Gibbon's attention to the importance of the placement of notes. When the first volume of *The*

Gibbon: Gentleman of Letters (Baltimore and London: The Johns Hopkins University Press, 1982), p. 127. It should be said—with regret perhaps, but also with some asperity—that Craddock has not been well served by her publishers. Citations are unconscionably abbreviated and squeezed into parentheses that disfigure the text: (M 247), for example. A trip to "Abbreviations" at the front of the book is required to learn that *M* stands for Murray's *Autobiographies of Edward Gibbon* and not Gibbon's *Memoirs* —unless one's own *M,* that is, *memory,* is exceptional. For Craddock's commentary notes we are trundled off to the end of the book. When found (a difficult task; see my note 52, page 86), these notes often have a reference that necessitates a journey back to the front of the book. Scholarly work is already circuitous enough without Johns Hopkins's mazy addition; that it occurs in the biography of England's best-known footnoter suggests a lack of taste as well as an absence of thoughtfulness.

38. Patricia B. Craddock, *Edward Gibbon: Luminous Historian, 1772–1794* (Baltimore and London: The Johns Hopkins University Press, 1989), p. 8.
   39. Ibid., p. 93.
   40. Ibid.

History appeared, its notes in the back, Hume reacted immediately. "One is . . . plagued with his Notes," he wrote
Gibbon's publisher—who happened also to be Hume's—"according to the present Method of printing the Book: When a
note is announced, you turn to the End of the Volume; and
there you often find nothing but the Reference to an
Authority: All these Authorities ought only to be printed at
the Margin or the Bottom of the Page."[41] Hume's advice
stimulated Gibbon; it did not guide him. Gibbon made no
use of the margins for his notes in future volumes, nor did he
leave his commentary to languish in the back of the book,
bringing only the references (as Hume suggested) to the bottom of the page. Every note became a footnote; and we
should first celebrate and then explain his perfect judgment.
We need to get into Gibbon's head. In doing so we cannot
avoid speculation simply from fear of embarrassing ourselves
in front of Clio.

   Gibbon was an English parliamentarian. He took his seat at
a time when the first substantial threat to the British Empire
was rolling in from the American colonies. Tea was dumped;
Concord was marched toward and retreated from; General
Washington rowed as quietly as he could across the Delaware:
all of that during the days Gibbon listened to the back and
forth of debate, the verbal cut and thrust of master politicians, the hems and haws of the timid, the catcalls and catty
whispers of the backbenchers. The first volume of *The History*
came out in 1776, and soon after came Hume's suggestion.

---

41. Quoted in Anthony Grafton, *The Footnote: A Curious History*
(Cambridge, Mass.: Harvard University Press, 1997), p. 103. Grafton practices a kind of truncated footnoting that reflects, I think, the scholarly
bias of his view of footnotes. His citation reads: *"The Letters of David
Hume,* ed. J. Y. Greig (Oxford, 1932), II, 313."

Surely Gibbon, reminded of the possibilities of footnotes, was influenced by the temper of the times and the seating arrangements of the Parliament. We can let Gibbon think of his text as a prime minister's oration without too much stretching of the facts. He certainly would not want his notes to remain backbenchers; nor would he want them to be leaning over into the face of the orator, as they would be were the notes to be placed in the page margins. They needed to be at the bottom of the page. There they occupy the contradictory place of the leaders of the opposition: at a distance but close at hand. Someone once said that notes ran along the bottom of Gibbon's pages like dogs yapping at the text;* a more accurate depiction would have them leaping up like offended opposition leaders objecting or quibbling or dragging the debate off in a new direction.

Gibbon knew that it was the comments and not just the dry facts that enlivened parliamentary debate and persuaded the doubtful. His genius is never more evident than when he refuses to follow Hume toward a footnote of crabbed scholarship, and instead lets the footnote remain fulsome and varied and human. To know Gibbon's footnotes is to know Gibbon, the man.

He was a man of inexhaustible curiosity. When his text arrives at Commodus's rule, it has plenty to say about that cruel and strange emperor; and Gibbon makes sure to use the goings-on in the amphitheater to exhibit Commodus's dreadful taste for the slaughter of people and animals. A panther is dropped by a well-placed arrow before a cheering crowd, elephants, rhinoceros, a hundred lions. But when Commodus

---

* The source of this quotation eludes me. To ask readers for help is one of the best uses to which a footnote can be put. Ignorance is as much a part of scholarship as knowledge; both should be *acknowledge*d.

cuts "asunder the long bony neck of the ostrich . . . ,"[42] Gibbon
can't leave it at that. The reader, he assumes, is as desirous as
himself for details. "The ostrich's neck is three feet long, and
composed of seventeen vertebrae. . . ."[43] Not just a fox or a
pheasant has been killed but a splendid oddity. Gibbon knows
his compatriots. Beasts seen by Englishmen only in works of
art or in their "fancy," he emphasizes. The giraffe is one such
animal; Gibbon makes sure we know the giraffe is "the tallest,
the most gentle, and the most useless of the large quadrupeds."
Again the details: ". . . a native only of the interior parts of
Africa, [it] has not been seen in Europe since the revival of letters, and though M. de Buffon . . . has endeavored to describe,
he has not ventured to delineate, the giraffe."[44] But much
more is going on in this note than the supplying of details.
Under cover of adding information, Gibbon is rendering a
judgment. The description "tallest," "gentle," and "most useless" turns the fabled giraffe into an eccentric aunt whose visits to the house are as pleasant as they are rare; Commodus

---

42. Edward Gibbon, *The History of the Decline and Fall of the Roman Empire*
(London: Methuen, 1896), vol. I, p. 94. From the many editions of the
History, I have chosen the one edited by J. B. Bury. It is a classic edition,
of course, but its compact format, into which so many footnotes and
marginality are given just enough but not more space than absolutely
necessary, may alert the reader unfamiliar with Gibbon as to exactly how
magnificent was his accomplishment. Not only did he master the voluminous and unreliable sources of Rome's history, not only did he manage to lay down parallel after parallel sentence with scarcely a dull
paragraph—or at least without an entirely dull page—but he did it at a
time when London lacked public libraries and when publishers lacked
the resources that those of today often enjoy, and who were always
tempted to make the page do more than it comfortably can do. One is
hard pressed to choose Gibbon's primary virtue: his resilience, his reliability, or his readability.

43. Ibid., note 35.

44. Ibid., note 36.

has been turned into a contemptible bully—as well as a murderer.

Gibbon's "facts" often fly as swiftly and deadly as Commodus's arrows. When his text awhile later wanders into a discussion of the origins of English words, he uses a footnote to settle an old score. "Dr. Johnson affirms that *few* English words are of British extraction. Mr. Whitaker, who understands the British language, has discovered more than *three thousand,* and actually produces a long and various catalogue. . . ."[45] The quiet, invidious comparison of the tic-afflicted dictionary maker who "affirms" an error with Mr. Whitaker who "understands" the language is a fine example of speech as a whip that members of Parliament employed time and again. The italicizing of *"few"* and *"three thousand"* are the raised eyebrows of an experienced orator making sure his colleagues appreciate his point. Making the reader aware of a catalog is rubbing it in, but then Dr. Johnson was not known for his tact or his restraint either.*

The eighteenth century was an age of specialists if we judge it by its criminal class, which was made up of subdivision after subdivision of minute distinctions between different kinds of thieves and con men. But the literati were an exception. They refused specialization. A historian like Gibbon felt he

45. Edward Gibbon, *The History of the Decline and Fall of the Roman Empire* (London: Methuen, 1896), vol. IV, p. 153, note 151.

* Gibbon wasn't about to let his *bête noire* rest with just one sour note. Several volumes later, immersed in the Crusades when so much un-Christian behavior was exercised on behalf of Christian doctrine, a note turns the reader to Shakespeare's *Henry IV* for a more genuine and appropriate expression of love for country and mayhem. Fair enough, until he manufactures an excuse to refer to Dr. Johnson's edition of the play, and to Dr. Johnson's own notes, "the workings of a bigoted though vigorous mind, greedy of every pretense to hate and persecute those who dissent from his creed."

had as much right to lay down the law about derivations as about the succession of royalty; he pronounced with equal confidence on military strategy and on an ostrich's anatomy. Footnotes encouraged this expansiveness; the bottom of the page becomes a long, winding corridor where the scholar pops out of his office to stretch his legs and, meeting colleagues, gossips, tells jokes, rants about politics and society, and feels free to offer opinions based on nothing but his prejudices and whims. In this corridor the scholar becomes autodidact.

Gibbon himself opens the door and critiques Petrarch's verse: "He spins this allegory beyond all measure or patience."[46] And as poets are on his mind, Gibbon doesn't hesitate to spout off about one of his pet peeves, the office of poet laureate; he mutters about how poets often have been "false and venal" and then sputters "but I much doubt whether any age or court can produce a similar establishment of a stipendiary [sic] poet who in every reign and at all events, is bound to furnish twice a year a measure of praise and verse, such as may be sung in the chapel, and, I believe, in the presence of the sovereign."[47] To this point, the note might seem the casual aside a scholar makes to a colleague; however, Gibbon keeps the model of parliamentary oratory even when speaking in private. The personal is always political; the political always personal. So Gibbon clears his throat and continues. "I speak the more freely," he says, and we should imagine him bowing his head to the opposition humbly, "as the best time for abolishing this ridiculous custom is while the prince is a man of virtue and the poet a man of genius."[48] With this gra-

---

46. Edward Gibbon, *The History of the Decline and Fall of the Roman Empire* (London: Methuen, 1896), vol. VII, p. 281.

47. Ibid., p. 256.

48. Ibid.

cious *and* calculated compliment, Gibbon keeps the king and the poet laureate on his side of the aisle.

Gibbon took the picaresque footnote in hand and, without entirely breaking its spirit, put it into a suit. Under his tutelage, footnotes became trustworthy. They made pleasant dining companions. Their conversation is full of carefully balanced sentences and sudden quips, and they can be relied upon to use their napkins. Still, they remain various and filled with the unexpected, but also always with a public face. They are politicians even in the drawing room. To bring this home requires a digression of some length.*

Gibbon never cut a dashing figure in the eyes of the opposite sex and, in fact, suffered one disappointment after another. One of those disappointments cast a shadow over his entire life, affecting even his footnotes. The affair began simply enough in Switzerland when the twenty-year-old Gibbon met another twenty-year-old, Mademoiselle Curchod, a blond, blue-eyed "belle of Lausanne,"[49] coquettish *and* well read; it progressed when Suzanne, looking past the short and unprepossessing first impression of a mediocre dancer, saw a "physiognomy so extraordinary that one does not tire of examining it, of painting it, of copying it";[50] Gibbon, screwing up his courage, went off to England to tell his hardheaded father his son intended to marry a foreigner with no dowry and no prospects who had no intention of leaving her Switzerland

---

* Hume would have labeled this digression "commentary" and hustled it to the back of the book. But digression, as Bayle demonstrated conclusively, is as much a part of the thought process as a metaphor or a well-chosen example or, for that matter, logic's excluded middle, which Hume was so inordinately fond of.

49. Patricia B. Craddock, *Young Edward Gibbon: Gentleman of Letters* (Baltimore and London: The Johns Hopkins University Press, 1982), p. 107.

50. Ibid., p. 110.

after marriage. The affair came to an end with the young Gibbon dithering in England and Suzanne flirting with other men in Lausanne.[51]

Or rather, as is the case with so many early loves, it never really ended. Suzanne went on to become the wife of the formidable Jacques Necker, Swiss banker, Louis the Sixteenth's director general of finances and minister of state, and casualty of the French Revolution. A writer herself, she founded one of the first of the famous Parisian literary salons; her daughter became the extraordinary Madame de Staël, wit, novelist, and social historian. Gibbon became a member of Parliament, won European fame as the author of *The History of the Decline and Fall of the Roman Empire,* and settled into an unwanted and uncomfortable bachelorhood. They saw little of each other for a time.

No matter. When the first volume of *Decline and Fall* appears, Madame Necker scoops it up (presumably before it was translated into French). A letter from her soon arrives at Gibbon's London address filled with arguments and inducements for Gibbon to visit Paris and larded with thoughtful praise of his history. He has "immense erudition," she tells him, profound and precise "knowledge of men and humanity, of nations and individuals," and "a fertile and sensitive imagination."[52] She compares him to Tacitus, only in order to dis-

---

51. No love affair, however brief and however young the participants, can ever be summarized in a few lines. For a more complete, complicated, and painful account of this affair, see Patricia B. Craddock, *Edward Gibbon: Luminous Historian, 1772–1794* (Baltimore and London: The Johns Hopkins University Press, 1989), especially pp. 136-7, 156-7, 172-4.

52. See Patricia B. Craddock, *Edward Gibbon: Luminous Historian, 1772–1794* (Baltimore, London: The Johns Hopkins University Press, 1989), p. 84. Craddock is no better served by her publisher in this second volume of her luminous (to borrow the adjective she applies to Gibbon's

miss the Roman historian. "Only philosophers read Tacitus, you will be read by everyone. . . ." And then comes praise that, while couched as a general statement, subtly reveals a critic who once was in love: ". . . we shall learn to think while believing that we are only seeing and feeling."[53] Necker's response to the mature Gibbon's work usefully characterizes his prose but surely is also the response of a lover. The heightened alertness of the senses that accompanies love, and particularly first love, does often seem to become a way of knowing: Madame is visceral; her response is that of a woman remembering love. Gibbon had some intimations of this, for he "reread a hundred times" her "charming letter."[54] And he did make his way to Paris and her salon.

Madame Necker tempered her praise with some critical remarks, the most interesting of which, for our purposes, was the criticism of his treatment of women. "To hear you talk, all their virtues are artificial; were *you* the man, sir, who ought to have spoken so of women?"[55] This comment is not couched

---

work) biography than she was in her first volume. Note 10 in her text sends us to the back of the book where, under the general heading of "Notes to Pages 80–91," we find "10. Gibbon 1814, 2:177." To learn more we must proceed even further into the appendices' dungeon. Under the general heading of "Works Frequently Cited" and specifically under the entry for Gibbon, Edward, we are informed of a "——, 1814, *The Miscellaneous Works of Edward Gibbon.* Edited by John, Lord Sheffield. 5 vols. London: Cadell & Davies." The letter from Suzanne Necker is presumably part of that collection, but one feels less a scholar checking a source than a child sent out on a scavenger hunt by a baby-sitter who is particularly imaginative and resourceful.

53. Patricia B. Craddock, *Edward Gibbon: Luminous Historian, 1772–1794* (Baltimore and London: The Johns Hopkins University Press, 1989), p. 84.
54. Ibid.
55. Ibid., but be alert. The baby-sitting publisher's scavenger hunt leads us to a slightly different reference: Gibbon's *Miscellaneous Works,* 1814, 2:179, 178.

in merely general terms; some residue of personal resentment lingers. Gibbon responds as soon as possible; with the very next edition he inserts a new footnote into his first volume, one that goes out of its way to praise the wife of a particularly unpleasant emperor. That emperor, Maximin, did not simply exile or execute his enemies; some were crudely clubbed to death, others were turned over to wild beasts, but others, most imaginatively, were "sewed up in the hides of slaughtered animals." But Empress Paulina, the footnote claims, "sometimes brought back the tyrant to the way of truth and humanity."[56] A further exculpatory effort was made by the former wooer in subsequent volumes when he portrayed "female virtues more generously,"[57] a fact Gibbon made sure to point out to his Suzanne.

The hopes of the young Gibbon and the young Curchod, their subsequent disappointments and resentments, the lingering attraction to each other that both of them clearly felt, none of that would interest us now except for the light it cast on Gibbon's annotative habits. The personal and political are joined, the private and the public faces indistinguishable. Our picaresque footnote has become, like Tom Jones, an English squire. Now he is prepared to become a scholar under the tutelage of Leopold von Ranke. This unfortunate development comes next.

---

56. Ibid., note 12.
57. Ibid., p. 84.

5

The Illusion of Empire

THE EMPIRE BUILDERS of nineteenth-century England took enormous satisfaction in their work; they could walk up to their library's globe of the earth, spin it, and see that their labors of mind and body encircled it. Everywhere lay the outlines of British colonies or ex-colonies. "The sun never sets, harrumph harrumph, on the British Empire!" the globe spinner might say, and the port-splashed, contented voice would be the same as the one used to admire a gourmand's ten-course meal or a fine cigar. To such well-fed men the disintegration of the Empire was scarcely conceivable; it was everywhere and forever.

Footnotes would have occasioned similar contented voices should the men have browsed through their library, trailing wisps of smoke, pulling out and opening books at random: Lord Macaulay's *History of England,* perhaps, or Lieutenant Colonel Mundy's *Our Antipodes: Residence and Rambles in The Australasian [sic] Colonies with A Glimpse of the Gold Fields,* or Miss Jane Porter's romance, *Scottish Chiefs*—though one supposes empire builders might not be interested in heroic Scots. Still, Miss Porter's work saw international success, and was even published in the former colonies of America so a copy might find its way into a library of the upper class. In any case, these and the other books in any well-heeled English gentleman's library would attest that footnotes were everywhere: "The sun harrumph, etc., etc."

These days, of course, we are more impressed with the fall of empires than with their rise, and, indeed, the decline of the footnote's scope and power began even as it appeared most securely triumphant—surely typical of empires.

One man's name particularly deserves to be affixed to the footnote's decline: Leopold von Ranke.* Ranke was a scholar *and* a German, two terms that became nearly synonymous in the nineteenth century. He was devoted to research; one of his readers has said that Ranke's prefaces to his books were "enthusiastic travel reports by a traveler who visited, not city after city, but library after library."[1] Ranke himself makes clear that he preferred burrowing among dark archives to idly drinking and taking in the sun in some outdoor café. "How quickly one studies the day away," he crooned, as if he were an archivist's Wordsworth and documents were so many daffodils.[2] Like every scholar, however, he developed a complicated relationship with footnotes; he needed them, of course, but he resisted them when he could and, at times, sabotaged

---

* Ranke after a time became a firm supporter of the footnote; but his policies, if not his intentions, undid the footnote, as we will see. His subconscious must take some of the blame.

1. Peter Gay, *Style in History* (New York: Basic Books, 1974), p. 74.

2. L. von Ranke, *Idas Brifwerk,* ed. W. P. Fuchs (Hamburg, 1949), p. 194. Quoted in Anthony Grafton, *The Footnote: A Curious History* (Cambridge, Mass.: Harvard University Press, 1997), p. 36. (Grafton's annotation is not as fulsome as one might wish, as I indicated before.) With Ranke, Grafton gives another one of those succinct tour-de-force descriptions of a life, work, and personality that appear throughout *The Footnote.* I have borrowed a great number of his facts and antidotes; our interpretations of them differ dramatically: For the most part, he approves of what happened to the footnote in Ranke's hands; I entirely disapprove.

them. Early on he told his publisher that he included citations only because a young author needed to prove his reliability but that he had "carefully avoided going in for real
annotation."[3] He once meticulously counted up the footnotes in a predecessor's chapters in order to show that the citations could convey a false sense of scholarly support—
twenty-seven references in chapter 104, he tells us, and twenty-
seven more references to the same source in chapter 105. All
fifty-four footnotes send us to the same source, and a doubtful one at that.

The unreliable annotator Jean Charles Leonard Sismonde
de Sismondi was Swiss, not German, and used French as a
first language, but Ranke's purpose was clearly to raise general questions about the effectiveness of citations and not
just about the reliability of non-German scholarship.[4]

To write history *"wie es eigentlich gewesen,"*[5] or "history as it
had really been," was Ranke's credo, or at least the credo that
subsequent historians (who also presumably wanted their accounts to be *"wie es eigentlich gewesen"*) decided was Ranke's.

---

3. G. Stanton Ford, "A Ranke Letter," *Journal of Modern History* 32 (1960),
p. 143. Quoted in Anthony Grafton, *The Footnote: A Curious History*
(Cambridge, Mass.: Harvard University Press, 1997), p. 64. Many writers,
and particularly many scholarly writers, might not feel the need to repeat the Grafton citation in full even though the reader may have to
hunt a bit for it. That parsimony is a mistake. Notes should be reader-
friendly; a book should not emulate a supermarket in which the bread is
at one end of the store and another common purchase—say, cheese—is at
the other. A reader is not a customer who may buy on impulse if required to wander the store (or story). When in doubt, footnote fully.

4. For a full account of this episode, see Anthony Grafton, *The Footnote:
A Curious History* (Cambridge, Mass.: Harvard University Press, 1997),
pp. 40–4.

5. Ranke, *Tagebucher,* p. 233. Quoted in Peter Gay, *Style in History* (New
York: Basic Books, 1974), p. 68. Gay's citations can be as terse as
Grafton's.

Ranke wanted to be "scientific, perhaps"; certainly he hoped to be accurate. A well-qualified contemporary historian has argued, however, that Ranke was just as concerned to provide a good tale as to provide scientific authority. ". . . Ranke's free employment of dramatic devices," Peter Gay writes, "places him in the camp of those historians who treat their craft as a branch of the storytelling art."[6] Unfortunately, Ranke failed to see the dramatic possibilities of footnotes; to him, they were simply interruptions required by the exigencies of the historian's craft, a failure of imagination that him led him to adopt several questionable practices.

First, he apparently did not always try to put his footnotes where they would clearly indicate the source of his facts and judgments; instead, he tried to hold off annotating until he came to a place where a note would not break the flow of his narrative. An exasperated reader called him on that. The reader complained that such consolidation of notes and the delay in their insertion made for imprecise annotation; Ranke's book was "inchoate, sentimental" and mostly would please only "learned ladies."[7] Ranke grumbled a reply in a

6. Peter Gay, *Style in History* (New York: Basic Books, 1974), p. 64.

7. Quoted in Anthony Grafton, *The Footnote: A Curious History* (Cambridge, Mass.: Harvard University Press, 1997), p. 66. In one library copy of *The Footnote* I found scrawled in pencil after "learned ladies" a sarcastic "Thanks a lot." The writer, presumably a woman, was quite justified. Though the long-dead Leo will not benefit, other readers, myself included, can only benefit from the highlighting of such egregious sexism. In a wonderfully digressive footnote, Grafton goes from Ranke's note-taking to the Renaissance historian Jacob Burckhardt's note-taking to the suggestion: "Next to the unwritten history of annotation that haunts historical libraries' walls is the ghost of the even thicker history of note-taking. . . ." (p. 46, note 19). Such a history ought to pay some attention to the *note making* of anonymous readers who in a more modern age imitate the commentary found scrawled on medieval manuscripts.

footnote: "I cite for those who want to find, but not for those who look in order *not* to find."[8] He did not explain why any scholar should fail to make it as easy as possible to find the source of a quotation; a scholar's research surely should not be game of hide-and-seek—though a sense of play and a child's capacity to wonder (and wander) are essential to the scholar, of course.

Ranke also took to sequestering much of his most interesting commentary at the end of a book. His multivolume *History of the Popes,* for example, allocates 274 of its 1,205 pages or about 10 percent of its space to 165 appendices. No one would argue that all of that material should be run along the bottoms of the pages, but some of it clearly should. To give one demonstration: The Council of Trent, as Ranke says, "engrosses a large portion of the history of the sixteenth century";[9] indeed, his *History of the Popes* necessarily keeps returning to it. Ranke draws on two accounts of it, which are "directly opposed to each other,"[10] one of them by a certain Paolo Sarpi and the other by Pallavicini. At the time Ranke wrote no consensus had been reached as to whose word was more to be trusted; some church historians called Sarpi mendacious and Pallavicini honest, some reversed the adjectives. Sorting this out might well have been confined to an appendix, particularly if the publisher happens to be a parsimonious type; but surely the personal interpolation that occurs

8. L. Ranke, "Replik," *Intelligenzblatt der Allgemeinen Literatur-Zeitung* 131 (May 1828), cols. 193–199, at 195–196 n. Quoted in Anthony Grafton, *The Footnote: A Curious History* (Cambridge, Mass.: Harvard University Press, 1997), p. 66. English translation by Grafton.

9. Leopold von Ranke, *History of the Popes: Their Church and State,* vol. 3, trans. E. Fowler (New York and London: The Co-Operative Publication Society, 1901), p. 220.

10. Ibid.

in the appendix of Ranke's deserves to be directly under the text: "On approaching these voluminous works [Pallavicini's and Sarpi's], we are seized with a sort of terror."[11] Nothing in any of the restrained, entirely professional footnotes that accompany Ranke's text on the Council of Trent does the job of this single sentence. The reader cannot escape its clear warning of troubled waters ahead; to stick it in the back of the book is the scholarly equivalent of dragging a lighthouse well into the interior so its flashing beacon will not disrupt the smooth sailing of pleasure cruises. Ranke continues for several paragraphs more, emphasizing just how "formidable" is his "task rendered by the fact we have to be on our guard at every step, lest we should be falsely directed by one or the other, and drawn into a labyrinth of intentional deceptions!"[12] No sentence that earns an exclamation point should be kept at a distance from the text; nor should the appendix be summing up: "Even in these folios, from which industry itself recoils in terror, the presence of a poet makes itself felt."[13] To move from terror to poetry in the space of a few paragraphs is a splendid sleight of hand; it should be done center stage, not backstage.* Nothing makes clearer that the historian's facts are melted by interpretation on the skillet of the writer's temperament.

---

11. Ibid., p. 220.

12. Ibid., p. 221.

13. Ibid.

* A single citation could have been inserted at the end of this paragraph; some writers, pulling Ranke, would have done just that. However, making the author work rather than the reader is a firm principle of this book even at the risk of unnecessary duplication. Judgment is required, of course; for example, no citation was given for the single word *formidable,* an elision some might regret.

We should not be dogmatic. When an asterisk is affixed to a paragraph about a relatively insignificant event—an invasion of Poland, for example, of which there have been so many— and when the asterisk takes us to a footnote saying simply, "See Appendix, Nos. 66, 67, and 68,"[14] and when appendix no. 66 begins, "I find nothing to add to the contents of these documents, which I have already used for the text. . . ."[15]—well, even the most devoted fan of the footnote might think this is one the author could have skipped.

Ranke's reputation spread to England and America and around the world. The *History of the Popes* was translated into English five separate times in the nineteenth century. The American Historical Association elected him its first honorary member. George Bancroft, the great American historian, called him "the greatest living historian." "Probably no historian in the nineteenth century," it has been said more recently, "has had an influence on the development of historical scholarship equal to that of Leopold von Ranke."[16] Unfortunately, this means his influence on the footnote has been nearly as great; gradually scholars have adopted Ranke's restricted view of notes. The loss it entailed should be emphasized with an example. Both Ranke and that earlier, formidable annotator Pierre Bayle happened to have covered the

---

14. Leopold von Ranke, *History of the Popes: Their Church and State*, vol. 2, trans. E. Fowler (New York and London: The Co-Operative Publication Society, 1901), p. 265.

15. Ibid.

16. See the editor's forward to Leopold von Ranke, *The Theory and Practice of History*, ed. Georg G. Iggers and Konrad von Moltke (Indianapolis and New York: Bobbs-Merrill, 1973), p. vii. Note also Grafton's comment ". . . Ranke became the academic historian par excellence. . . ." Anthony Grafton, *The Footnote: A Curious History* (Cambridge, Mass.: Harvard University Press, 1997), p. 34.

career of David, the Goliath slayer. Bayle does it in about ten
of his expansive pages devoted to the biblical hero—pages that
generate ten extended footnotes easily employing more words
than the text itself. Branching off from the text and the footnotes are some fifty-five margin notes, most of them citations
of sources but a few providing additional commentary. The
drama created by such a multiplicity of voices has been
demonstrated before, but a small reminder might be in order.

After the beheading of Goliath, Saul had to ask a general for
the name of the Israelites' hero, according to Bayle's reading of
the Bible. Immediately, Bayle in effect shakes his head in disbelief. Reference mark [f] takes us to the margin for a brief citation; [B] takes us to commentary at the bottom of the page.
Our own head bobs, mimicking the gesture of disbelief and,
more important, reinforcing it. [B] is a typical, sly digression of
Bayle's. "It is somewhat strange that Saul did not know David
that Day," the footnote begins, "since that young Man had
[played] several times on his Musical Instruments before him,
to disperse those black Vapours *[sic]* that molested him."[17]
Thus the shake of the head: but of course Bayle doesn't leave it
at that; Bayle goes after his source, the Bible, by indirection. "If
such a Narrative as this should be found in Thucydides . . . all
the critics would unanimously conclude, that the Transcribers
had transposed the Pages, forgot something in one Place, repeated something in another, or inserted some preposterous
Additions in the Author's name."[18] God's "word" has been
safely (or somewhat safely) put in doubt at a time when reli-

---

17. Peter *[sic]* Bayle, *The Dictionary, Historical and Critical* (London:
printed for J. J. and P. Knapton; D. Midwinter; J. Brotherton; A.
Bettesworth, C. Hitch . . . [and 25 others], 1734–1738), 2nd ed., vol. 2, p.
606, note [C]. Let me remind the reader that *S*'s have been modernized.
18. Ibid.

gious belief was a matter of life and death; the double standard that some of Bayle's colleagues used when considering biblical and classical sources has been challenged at a time when scholarly disputes could turn violent. [C] continues on for some further length, but the point is made; Bayle has once again used the footnote to stir the dramatic pot.

Compare Ranke's single footnote with his ten pages on David—pages that admittedly are lacking the space afforded Bayle. As the text follows David's triumphant rise to power and his tumultuous rule over the Israelites, a single footnote appears. This note likewise questions authority and in its way is useful, but it saps the drama of the moment instead of increasing it. An Amalekite appears before David to inform him of Saul's death; the Amalekite admits that "at the fallen king's entreaty, he had given him the death-blow."[19] For that, the overly honest messenger is put to death himself. An asterisk pops up. "As is well known, there is at this point, between the accounts in the last chapter . . . ," the dry voice of the scholar begins, and one pays attention to only bits of it, really as if a bored mechanic were explaining just what had been fixed in your car—you know it's important to listen but how the voice drones—"certain discrepancy . . . somewhat arbitrary expedient . . . a pretended claim. . . ."[20] One simply wants to jump into one's car and drive briskly home—or in this case to jump back into the narrative and find out where David is headed next.

---

19. Leopold von Ranke, *The Oldest Historical Group of Nations and the Greeks*, ed. G. W. Prothero (New York: Harper & Brothers, 1985), p. 44. This, of course, is a translation, the only volume of three to be published in English.

20. Ibid., note.

Ranke lacks the true annotator's flair; his voice becomes distant, less animated when he descends to the bottom of the page. Scholars imitated Ranke, unfortunately, as the nineteenth century moved into the twentieth; their desire to appear scientific gradually undermined the notion of wide-ranging footnotes able to fit into the narrative of a novel as well as of a history, notes that could be as important to a casual memoir as to a scientific report, that were willing to play a starring role or a character part or a walk-on, and that refused to be typecast. Not that other models were unavailable; they could be found scattered over half the globe.

Another German of the same era, Wolfgang Menzel, was keeping the annotating slyness of Gibbon very much alive. Menzel had brought out a three-volume *History of Germany, from the Earliest Period to the Present Time* well before Ranke had finished his *Nine Books of Prussian History;* its footnotes remain a delight. When he arrives at the Seven Years' War, the German historian takes great satisfaction in a French defeat, to the point of gloating. "The Prussians take ten thousand prisoners," he tells us, but the "booty chiefly consisted in objects of gallantry belonging rather to a boudoir than to a camp." That would have satisfied most celebrants, but Menzel adds, "The French army perfectly resembled its mistress, the Marquise de Pompadour."[21] A fear of appearing smug may have moved Menzel to pause; he inserts an asterisk. Below, the footnote introduces us to a certain Seidlitz, a Prussian "who covered himself with glory on this occasion. . . ." He was "the best horseman of the day." An unexceptional note, so far, but then with one sentence, one brief digression, Menzel changes

---

21. Wolfgang Menzel, *The History of Germany, from the Earliest Period to the Present Time,* vol. 3, trans. Mrs. George Horrocks (London: Henry G. Bohn, 1849), p. 62.

everything: "[Seidlitz] is said to have once ridden under the sails of a windmill when in motion."[22] The war, a bloody, futile, ugly war, has been turned into a kind of odd sporting event of horsemanship and obstacle courses. Our perspective shifts for a moment; making fun of the French becomes just the high spirits of a winning tennis player running up to the net, shouting, or a defensive back trash-talking his tackled opponent.*

Not much later, in the United States, another historian, John S. C. Abbott, also used footnotes to good advantage. The Civil War had ended just two years before when Abbott managed to put out a history of it, a history whose pages are filled with asterisks, daggers, and double daggers. The war is covered briskly, and soon the Blue and the Gray arrive at Gettysburg, the Union digs in, Joshua Chamberlain, the dour professor, and his Maine brigade hold on to Little Round Top, the flamboyant Pickett and his division make their famous charge, and then there are the dead to be buried and the wounded to be tended. Abbott calculates that the scene shocks and depresses us. Perhaps we will turn away,† so he uses a footnote to dispel some of the gloom while keeping us "at war." A "red-cheeked,

22. Ibid., note, p. 62.

* Modern readers understandably may resist the reduction of war to sport; the example of a skilled use of footnotes remains. Menzel has Gibbon's ability to change our perspective with a single phrase or even a single word. Another footnote of his explains the ransom acquired by a French king: "The Spanish crown diamonds (an incredible number) were . . . sent to Paris. . . ." That parenthesis is such an exact exclamation of wonder, we (or the children within all of us) are actually there, standing on tiptoes, the better to see the jewels. Wolfgang Menzel, *The History of Germany, from the Earliest Period to the Present Time*, vol. 3, trans. Mrs. George Horrocks (London: Henry G. Bohn, 1849), p. 2.

† The details of the carnage have not been included here; they are unnecessary to make my point.

strong country girl" was asked if she was "'. . . frightened when the shells began flying?'" "'Well, no,' she said, 'you see we was all a-baking bread round here . . . and had our dough a-rising . . . I couldn't leave my bread.'" An officer tells her to go to the cellar but: "'I told him I *could not* leave my bread.'"[23]

In England, too, historians carried on the Gibbon annotating tradition; Lord Macaulay leaps to mind. Not a very sensible choice, many would immediately say, for Macaulay's reputation is tarnished; in fact, one entertaining essay on the historian begins with a list of great writers who could not stand the man: Thomas Carlyle, Walter Bagehot, Matthew Arnold, Lord Morley, Sir Leslie Stephen, Sir Charles Firth. A list of condemning adjectives follows: *verbose, artificial, overemphatic, wearisome,* and, finally, just plain *irritating.* "With Macaulay," comes the conclusion of the case against him, "clarity somehow becomes a vice."[24]

---

23. John S. C. Abbott, *The History of the Civil War in America; Comprising a Full and Impartial Account of the Origin and Progress of the Rebellion of the Various Naval and Military Engagements, of the Heroic Deeds Performed By Armies and Individuals, and of Touching Scenes in the Field, the Camp, the Hospital, and the Cabin,* vol. 2 (New York: Ledyard Bill, 1866), note, p. 414, italics in the original. The original source is given as simply: *"What We Did at Gettysburg,* p. 14." The story is introduced in a way that might make contemporary readers long for that female reader of Grafton's work who did not let pass a sexist remark. (From a cited source, not Grafton's own words, I should remind the reader.) See above, note 7, page 92.

24. Peter Gay, *Style in History* (New York: Basic Books, 1974), pp. 97–8. This present writer confesses to a certain fondness for Macaulay that might make it too easy to forgive his faults. In my first year of college, I had an English teacher who was devoted to the historian. He spent two terms drumming into our heads the beauty of the balanced sentence. I turned out to have some facility at that narrow part of styling: If I mentioned black birds in the snow, I quickly revised the phrase to "black birds in the white snow." If I gave three examples of poor behavior of kings of England, I would follow it with three, not two or four, examples

Macaulay *was* a talker—something also held against him, though not by me. A Sydney Smith reported a dream in which he "was chained to a rock and being talked to death by Harriet Martineau and Macaulay."[25] Good talkers, though, have a high tolerance for digression and quips, and Macaulay's notes delight us with both. In *History of England* he lets himself go on a bit too long about the minting of money; he may have noticed some of his listeners' eyelids half closed. Abruptly a footnote clears its throat and says loudly and opinionatedly: "The first writer who notices the fact that, when good money and bad money are thrown into circulation together, the bad money drives out the good money, was Aristophanes." A sudden change, in this case the leap from Restoration England to the great age of Greece, inevitably wakens an audience, "Aristophanes?" a drifting mind asks, and the eyes open wide. That's a trick known by any two-bit orator, but Macaulay is much more than that; he uses the newly honed attention to make an unexpected point. Aristophanes attributes his fellow citizens' preference for bad money to their bad taste, or so Macaulay claims; this allows him to say: "But, though his political economy will not bear examination, his verses are excellent. . . ."[26] Notice the sly innuendo employed by this nineteenth-century Whig, one of England's most fervent patriots; "verses are excellent," this at a time when the Greek classics were idolized by most

---

of good behavior. The A that teacher delightedly gave me was one of the few I received at that institution, perhaps the reason I am reluctant to accept that Macaulay is "verbose" or "irritating."

25. R. K. Webb, *Harriet Martineau: A Victorian Radical* (1960), p. 11. Quoted in Peter Gay, *Style in History* (New York: Basic Books, 1974), p. 127. (Gay is responsible for the abbreviated citation to Webb.)

26. *The Works of Lord Macaulay: History of England*, vol. VI (London: Longman's, Green, 1898), p. 89, note 2.

college-educated Englishmen. But "excellent" puts Aristophanes in his place; the country of Shakespeare and Tennyson is not going to take a backseat to anyone while Macaulay is in charge. Is it too glib to suggest that Macaulay's genius, as this footnote demonstrates, was to combine balanced sentences with unbalanced enthusiasms?

That there were historians who offered an alternative to the restrictive annotating practices of Ranke is easy to demonstrate; we must not stop there, however. Footnotes should never be viewed only as a scholarly tool to be used by professionals.

Richard F. Burton, though a clear and entertaining story-teller, was not a professional writer by any means; he was a professional soldier, a British lieutenant stationed in Bombay. In the middle of the nineteenth century Lieutenant Burton volunteered to trek through the eastern and central regions of Arabia, at the time a "huge white blot"[27] on English maps, and to sneak into "El-Medinah" [sic] and "Meccah" [sic] in disguise. A disguise requires imitation, and imitation requires—if it is to succeed as it did for Burton—close observation of habits; for Burton the footnote became a place where exquisitely detailed observations could be exhibited like exotic footwear or fragile mummies in a glass case without cluttering up the narrative adventures of the text.

Arab friends in the text sneer at his poor-looking "copper-cased watch";[28] the text takes no notice but continues on to his sextant, the ownership of which turns out to be a near dis-astrous mistake. Sextants would be carried only by "infidels

27. Richard F. Burton, *Personal Narrative of a Pilgrimage to El-Medinah and Meccah* (New York: G. P. Putnam, 1956), p. 17.
28. Ibid., p. 112.

from India,"[29] a "young Meccan rogue, Mohammed,"[30] insists. Readers like myself will also continue on with the narrative until we are sure Burton is safe from discovery, in this case thanks to the intervention and vigorous advocacy of an influential Arab friend. Only then will we turn back to the watch and admire the careful footnote it occasions. A watch "being an indispensable instrument for measuring distances," Burton explains in the note, "I had it divested of gold case, and provided with a facing carefully stained and figured with Arabic numerals. . . . The watches worn by respectable people in El Hefaz are almost always old silver pieces, of the turnip shape, with hunting cases and an outer *etui* of thick leather. . . ."[31]

The art of this kind of annotation, of adding information without interrupting the pleasure of the story, demands a finely tuned sense of timing and of narrative *pull;* the pull must be strong enough to carry the reader past the reference mark, but a pause in the story, a diminishing of excitement, must occur soon enough for the reader to remember the footnote and want to return to it.

Lieutenant Burton, the amateur writer, doesn't always get the balance right. Well into his travels, having arrived at some of the most holy places of the Moslems, at a time when the reader is conscious of the utmost peril for Burton, the lieutenant keeps his story going for the most part. Then he descends a flight of steps to a hall at the entrance of the Bab el Ziyadah. Here pilgrims must remove their slippers, ". . . it not

---

29. Ibid., p. 113.

30. Ibid., p. xiv. This characterization of Mohammed is by Bayard Taylor, who, caught up in the adventure, is harshly critical of someone threatening the hero; Burton himself is more judicious.

31. Ibid, pp. 112–3, note s.

being considered decorous to hold them when circumambu-
lating the Kaabah."[32] We are immersed in the exotic, danger-
tinged wonder of the culture, when an asterisk sends us to
"An old pair of slippers is here what the 'shocking bad hat' is
at a crowded house in Europe, a self-preserver. Burckhardt [a
previous European pilgrim] lost three pair. I, more fortunate
or less wealthy, only one."[33] A nice bit of cultural translation,
perhaps, a useful reminder that all countries have their
thieves, but do we really want to be awakened from the nearly
dreamlike foreignness in which the text has enveloped us?

Another nonprofessional, E. H. Shackleton, the legendary
explorer, uses a footnote for the most extraordinary effect.
His account of his 1907–1909 journey to the South Pole has
almost no notes; the page bottoms are as featureless as ice
fields to the unobservant. Far into the account, Shackleton
describes with amazement the ability of life to survive in that
harsh cold. Stones are found "covered by bright red patches,
as though they had been sprinkled with blood."[34] Rotifers,
microscopic animals, somehow have survived the brutal climate; the excited explorers collected some to take back home.
Unfortunately, on the trip back to Australia the weather
turned nearly tropical for several weeks and the valuable animals "were found to be all dead when they reached Sydney."[35]
A sad business. But then one of the text's rare asterisks is encountered; its note informs us: "Since this was written, examination of the rotifers in London . . . has shown that they are
still living."[36] The brief moment we have between the text's

32. Ibid., p. 380.
33. Ibid., note.
34. E. H. Shackleton, *The Heart of the Antarctic; Being the Story of the British Antarctic Expedition 1907–1909* (London: William Heinemann, 1909), p. 237.
35. Ibid., p. 238.
36. Ibid., note.

obit and the note's correction, that brief lowering of the head, allows us to experience the disappointment of Shackleton's crew and then their elation, an experience we would have missed had the text simply been corrected. A sophisticated annotator is at work here.

There are also attempts to make use of the footnote in the novel, attempts not entirely satisfactory in some cases. Herman Melville and his *Moby-Dick* have become so famous we forget how easily he was dismissed while living in western Massachusetts, as he did much of the time. His house, a tourist attraction (and a short drive from where I happen to live), probably receives more visitors now than it did when he still occupied it. For such a marginal writer to use footnotes in his magnum opus required courage, and we should honor him for that. But the notes disappoint; they are not the notes of a novelist but of a pedant, if a strangely entertaining pedant at times.

An example: Moby-Dick has been found; Ahab and his crew have given chase in three small boats; the whale submerges and then rises, mouth agape, to smash the boat Ahab commands. Ahab is in the water, the novel is rushing toward one of its climaxes as Moby-Dick thrusts his head up and down while revolving his body at the same time. An asterisk intervenes. "This motion," the note unnecessarily tells us, "is peculiar to the sperm whale. It receives its designation (pitchpoling) from its being likened to that preliminary up-and-down poise of the whale-lance . . . ,"[37] but the reader can be spared the remaining two dozen words; the point is made.

Melville's annotating efforts have not been a total loss, however. Much earlier in the novel is a discussion of some of the

---

37. Herman Melville, *Moby-Dick, or The Whale* (Berkeley, Los Angeles, and London: University of California Press, 1981), p. 552. This edition is being used for reasons that soon will become obvious.

fierce habits of sperm whales; in a footnote Melville calls upon
a chief mate of a ship sunk by a whale to confirm the assault
was intentional. Some of what the mate has to say is affecting:
"The dark ocean and swelling waters were nothing . . . ," he says
at one point, "the dismal looking wreck, and *the horrid aspect
and revenge of the whale,* wholly engrossed my reflections. . . ."[38]
But this bit of emotion hardly merits calling special attention
to this note; the justification is what a twentieth-century artist
made of the nineteenth-century novelist. Barry Moser is the
artist. His 1979 edition of *Moby-Dick* inserts one of his engravings into the footnote itself. A malevolent black shape thrusts
across the page and stoves in a ship; the ship is pressed hard
against the illustration's frame, its hull compressing, its sails
collapsing: a wonderful picture that should encourage other
adventuresome artists to seek out footnotes as galleries for the
visual arts.

A much more popular novelist, Miss Jane Porter of
Scotland, lost her nerve employing footnotes. Her *The Scottish
Chiefs: A Romance,* which enjoyed for a time an international
readership,* has some tentative notes. Sir William Wallace
knights a follower and a note informs us that it takes three
"strokes" of the sword to accomplish this. The young man
gets up with "all the roses of his springing fame glowing in
his countenance. . . ." and almost immediately a note informs
us a new knight received a sword, spurs, and a girdle.[39] Other
footnotes are similar: terse, matter-of-fact, undramatic. An introduction suggests the reason for her timidity. She intended

---

38. Ibid., p. 209–10, note.
* Miss Porter mentions receiving letters from Vienna, Berlin, Moscow,
and India. Miss Jane Porter, *The Scottish Chiefs: A Romance* (New York:
Derby & Jackson, 1857), p. 23.
39. See ibid., p. 178, both text and two notes.

to use many more notes in order to assure us of the authenticity of the historical event occurring in her novel; but that would have required so many footnotes as to "swell each volume beyond its proper size."[40]

It rankles, this association of footnotes with scientific scholarship, and the tendency to restrict notes to mere citation that Ranke did so much to foster. As early as the 1850s it already had disarmed a popular novelist.

Fortunately, writers of other genres were not as easily intimidated. Some still used the footnote as a safe place for controversial material—apparently under the assumption that censorious types would assume notes simply cited sources or engaged in other unexceptional behavior. A biographer of Lafcadio Hearn put into a note reminiscences by a cousin that might have drawn clerical censure. The cousin recalls visiting Hearn at his "priest's college." She was taken upstairs "and on the way [he bade] me bow to an image of the Virgin, which I refused to do."[41] That refusal could have caused trouble, one supposes, but at the bottom of the page has the hope of being overlooked.

An equally telling example comes from a biographer of Henry Mackenzie, Esq. After nearly four hundred pages of Mackenzie's life and of his great admiration and fondness for Robert Burns, a footnote tells us, "Mackenzie's reverence for the memory of Burns did not prevent a playful use of the poet's name that was of doubtful taste." It seems that Mackenzie forged a Burns poem protesting the cutting down

---

40. Ibid., p. 22. She had some excuse for wishing to avoid controversy; *The Scottish Chiefs* along with works by Madame de Staël were banned in France at one time. See ibid., p. 23.

41. Elizabeth Bisland, *The Life and Letters of Lafcadio Hearn* (Boston and New York: Houghton Mifflin, 1906), p. 34, note 1.

of trees by "the old Duke of Queensberry" and read it before
the Royal Society of Edinburgh, giving out the story that the
poem had been found "pasted on a window shutter in an old
inn or tollhouse near the scene of the desolation."[42] (Those
unconversant with the Burns mythology may not understand
this tale's implication: Burns would have had to be falling-
down drunk to have disposed of a poem of his in this careless
way; he had a keen appreciation for the worth of his work.
Against all the evidence, Scots resent any hint that their great
poet's verse was inspired by booze.) The forgery made it into
one edition of Burn's complete works.

Anyone who has been present at one of the well-liquored fes-
tivities of Scotland's annual birthday party for "Bobby" Burns
knows what a sensitive issue a Burns forgery would be.
Tucking it away in a footnote would be the better part of valor.

A similar discretion probably accounts for some of the footnotes found in Harold Murdock's vivid telling of the battle of
Bunker Hill; Americans are as protective of their armed fore-
bears as Scots are of their tipsy poets. A participant in the fight
who had been up all night digging trenches complained in his
diary that they were supplied with ". . . but little victuals, no
Drink but Rum." A reference dagger takes us down immediately
to a note that begins: "This cannot be construed as the wail of
a teetotaler. The men were up and down from Charlestown
Village all the morning and had free access to the town wells.
What Brown yearned for was a long drink of the wine of the
country—that is cider and beer."[43] Murdock was writing during

---

42. Harold William Thompson, *A Scottish Man of Feeling: Some Account of
Henry Mackenzie, Esq. of Edinburgh and of the Golden Age of Burns and Scott*
(London and New York: Oxford University Press, 1931).

43. Harold Murdock, *Bunker Hill: Notes and Queries on a Famous Battle*
(Boston: Mifflin, 1927), p. 61, second note. Murdock's numerous footnotes deserve consideration by anyone interested in the art of annota-

the Prohibition era and knew the subject of rum and wine, however tactfully handled, would stir controversy; footnotes, like entrenchments, may require some extra work for the writer but also supply some cover from critical bombardments.

A book that appeared in 1901, *Last Words (Real and Traditional) of Distinguished Men and Women*, exemplifies the footnote as a depository of delicate matters. The author, Frederic Rowland Marvin, is scrupulous to a fault; notice the parenthetical qualification to the title. Marvin does not want any customer buying his work with the mistaken notion that he or she will be getting the unvarnished truth; no, some famous last words are apocryphal—buyer beware. The title then adds that the words are "collected from various sources"; and the reader quickly discovers that citations of sources are entirely absent. This is a no-nonsense book, and Marvin intends to make sure his word is trusted.

The lack of citations in *Last Words* does not mean there is a lack of footnotes; there are several formidable ones that demonstrate just how useful sophisticated annotation can be. The book opens with Dr. Alexander Adam, a headmaster at the "High School in Edinburgh," telling students, "It grows dark, boys. You may go."[44] It ends with the Swiss reformer Zwingle, as he receives a mortal wound in battle: "Well! they [sic] can, indeed, kill the body, but they are not able to kill the soul."[45] The prevailing tone of the pages in between has a similar decorum and seriousness as befits their subject; however,

---

tion; unfortunately, the edition to which I refer (and the only one as far as I am aware) was limited to 535 copies. No evidence has appeared to suggest that the footnotes were responsible for the publisher's parsimony, though it is natural to harbor suspicions.

44. Frederic Rowland Marvin, *The Last Words (Real and Traditional) of Distinguished Men and Women, Collected from Various Sources* (New York, Chicago, and Toronto: Fleming H. Revell, 1902), p. 1.

45. Ibid., p. 318.

not every famous person manages to die with dignity. Marvin, to his credit, is unwilling to distort the truth even as he works to maintain an appropriate tone. A footnote comes to his aid.

A Marcus of Arethusa, dying, says, heroically, "How am I advanced, despising you that are upon the earth." The manner of his death threatens his dignity, unfortunately, and, it has to be said, Marvin's tactful description just avoids being irreverent: Marcus, we are told, was "hung up in a basket smeared with honey" and "stung to death by bees. . . ."[46] Recognizing the peril in which his preferred tone has been placed by these words, Marvin sensibly puts in a footnote recognizing the fact. "To some of the most distinguished of our race death has come in the strangest possible way, and so grotesquely as to subtract greatly from the dignity of the sorrow it must certainly have occasioned."[47] The ordinary author would have stopped with those words; Marvin is made of much sterner stuff. He goes on to provide a brave array of other examples: the tyrant Agathocles succumbing to a poisoned toothpick; Anacreon choking to death on a dried grape; and the Roman praetor Fabius on a "single goat hair"; Aeschylus, the tragedian, killed when an eagle dropped a tortoise on his head; and a Prince of Wales felled by a cricket ball.[48]

The twentieth century has come upon our history with barely a nod from us, perhaps because we know it is a poor time for the footnote. Despite brave and imaginative annotators like Frederic Marvin, the worldwide "empire" of the footnote was as insecure as the British Empire—or for that matter

---

46. Ibid., p. 180.
47. Ibid., note 1.
48. Ibid.

any of the empires European nations put so much stock in. And in the same way that the Great War marks the beginning of the end of the domination of European countries, so too that disastrous war can conveniently mark the start of the footnote's decline—though many years were required for the implications of the decline to be felt.

By 1940 and the Second World War Edward Heron-Allen, gazing back on a life of annotation, was compelled to note with alarm that he might be one of the few, if not the only, genuinely passionate "foot-annotators" remaining.[49] His credentials for speaking out were impeccable. In 1900 his translation from the French of M. le Capitaine d'Arpentigny's commentary (itself a kind of extended footnote) on Chirognomy's already abundantly footnoted *La Science de la Main* managed to find a need for an additional 460 of Heron-Allen's own footnotes. And as he carefully explained, within those notes were further "note-signs" referring the reader "to the original Latin, Greek, French, German, . . . Italian, Arabic, Persian, and Turkish passages which occurred in the upper part of the [footnotes]."[50*] All of these were where one should expect genuine footnotes to be: at the foot of the page.

Unfortunately, Heron-Allen's 1928 book, *Barnacles in Nature and in Myth*, was not as well served by its publisher, the respectable but cost-conscious (by now) Oxford Press. Three hundred annotations assisting one hundred pages of text were sequestered at the end of the book. "Making referring

---

49. See Edward Heron-Allen, "Footnotes," *Notes and Queries*, 26 October 1940, p. 300.

50. Ibid., pp. 301-2.

* Edward Heron-Allen occasionally used the pseudonyms Christopher Blayre and Nora Helen Warddel. No evidence has been uncovered to suggest that he resorted to the changes in name in order to continue to use footnotes unimpeded.

to them very tiring," one reviewer said with unnecessary restraint.[*]

The shift in the status of the footnote already had been signaled by Hilaire Belloc back in 1923. That year his essay "On Footnotes" (slipped into his book *On*)[51][†] constructed an elaborate demonology with—appropriately enough—Edward Gibbon cast as the originator of evil.

Belloc begins simply; he calls Gibbon a liar. The evidence? A single lapse in which the historian mistakes Saint George, a reputable slayer of dragons, for a "corrupt, disgraceful bacon-contractor."[52] Gibbon relied on "a rubbish book of guess-work,"[53] a book Belloc was able to track down only because of a conveniently placed reference at the foot of Gibbon's text.

His success in correcting Gibbon's error does not make Belloc grateful to the footnote; on the contrary, instead of blaming the book that misled Gibbon, Belloc strikes out at the bearer of bad tidings, the helpful footnote. In fact, he insists that with this "evil footnote" Gibbon "introduced the first considerable serpent"[54] into some previously snake-free Eden of scholarship.

---

[*] The reviewer is full of admiration for *Barnacles in Nature and in Myth*. Unfortunately, he appears to place responsibility for the position of its footnotes upon Heron-Allen instead of upon the publisher, where it properly belongs. See George Sarton, "Edward Heron-Allen," *Isis,* vol. xii (May 1929), pp. 340–1.

51. Hilaire Belloc, *On* (New York: George H. Doran, 1923).

[†] The simplicity of many of Belloc's titles may be significant. In addition to *On*, he published *On Anything, On Everything, On Something, On Nothing & Kindred Subjects*. A general disdain for ornamentation of any kind may account for his particular dislike of footnotes.

52. Hilaire Belloc, *On* (New York: George H. Doran, 1923), p. 45.

53. Ibid.

54. Ibid., p. 43.

Having transformed Gibbon into Satan, Belloc claims for himself a role of similar stature. He will be the one to drive the footnote from the garden and put it at the end of the book, "in very small print indeed."[55]

Perhaps he succeeded; the publishing dates are suggestive.

> 1886: Heron-Allen's translation of M. le Capitaine d'Arpentigny appears; the footnotes are at the foot of the pages.
>
> 1923: Belloc's dramatic attack on the footnote appears.
>
> 1928: Heron-Allen's *Barnacles in Nature and in Myth* appears; its footnotes are banished by the Oxford University Press to the end of the book.

This may be rubbishy guesswork. Though Belloc graduated from Oxford, none of his considerable output was published by Oxford, nor is there evidence of any influence exerted by him on the university or the press. We also must recognize that the essays of Belloc can seldom be taken at face value. The casting of Gibbon as Satan and himself as the archangel Michael may have been facetious, a spoof of the misuse of biblical metaphor.*

While this was going on in England, a full-scale assault on the dignity of the footnote was mounted in the United States. Frank Sullivan's "A Garland of Ibids," the most widely read of the attacks, may have appeared first as an anonymous note in

---

55. Ibid., p. 51.

* As a Roman Catholic in Protestant England, Belloc's position must have been ambivalent at best. Though graduating honorably from Oxford University, he never attained the scholarly positions one might have expected—of course, it did not help that in addition to being a practicing Catholic, he was a practicing humorist.

The New Yorker,* whose urbane and unscholarly humorists were apparently hoping at that time finally to gain respectability by pretending to be literary. The short piece was then given weight and a broader readership by being included in a well-publicized anthology, *A Subtreasury of American Humor,* put out by two other employees of *The New Yorker.* (Even the Peoria bookstores and its library were likely to stock this anthology.) "A Garland" purports to be a review of Van Wyck Brooks's *New England: Indian Summer,* a book Sullivan purports to have read, though not much of its themes or critical judgments are evident in his piece. He purports even to have liked the book, though his "review" is one long whine about the book's numerous footnotes. "When you get to the footnote at the bottom of the page," he tells us at one point, as if footnotes were not by definition as well as custom at the bottom of the page, "like as not all you find is *ibid.*"[56] One of Sullivan's own typical, surly footnotes adds: "So is *cf.*"[57] Such is his scattershot criticism that he cannot, as

---

* This writer confesses he has not wandered back through the thickets of parodies and shopping hints *The New Yorker* consisted of before the war in order to pin down the first appearance of "The Garland of Ibids"; but the anthology thanks the magazine for the thing, and Frank Sullivan is known to have written many of its unsigned "Talk of the Town" pieces. So taken was Sullivan with *The New Yorker* and its suspect values that he once claimed to be the son of its famous editor, Harold W. Ross. The claim has Freudian significance at least, even if we assume that the brief bio in which it appeared was a spoof, as he also claimed in it to have authored a well-received novel titled *What Makes Martin Chuzzlewit Run.* See Frank Sullivan, *A Pearl in Every Oyster* (New York: Grosset & Dunlap, 1962), p. 291.

56. E. B. White and Katharine S. White, eds., *A Subtreasury of American Humor* (New York: Coward-McCann, 1941), p. 265.

57. Ibid., note 15. This writer is aware the previous note might well have been combined with this one; the temptation to show the convenience of the *ibid.* was too great, along with the demonstration that not much time is lost in moving the eyes from the text to the page bottom and back.

the present writer has tried to do, distinguish between the convenience of the *ibid.* and the inconvenience of the *cf.*

Strangely enough, a careful thumbing through of *New England: Indian Summer,* my eye glued to the bottoms of the pages, turned up neither a single *ibid.* nor a single *cf.*

Such slovenly research habits carry over into a much more important topic. Sullivan asks rhetorically, "How come writers of fiction do not need footnotes?" and adds, "Take Edna Ferber. She doesn't use footnotes."[58] Well, yes, Mr. Sullivan, the prosaic Ferber may not use notes, but surely (*we* might ask rhetorically) Mr. Sullivan has read Mr. Joyce. And you can't browse *Finnegan's Wake* for long without noticing the extravaganza of footnotes and margin notes that occurs a third of the way into the novel. Instead of Ferber, let Mr. Sullivan take just one of Joyce's footnotes—the first one to appear, for example: "Am shot, says the bigguard" in the text, and a footnote down below says, "Rawmeash, quoshe with her girlic teangue. If old Herod with the Comwell's eczema was to go for me like he does Snuffler whatever about his blue canaries I'd do nine months for his beaver beard."[59] Now, that is more

---

58. Ibid., (within text).

59. James Joyce, *Finnegan's Wake* (New York: Viking Press, 1974), p. 260, text and note 1. The poetic and footnote experimentation of *Finnegan's Wake* has never been successfully imitated; it has not been without influence, however. Lawrence Norfolk's recent novel *In the Shape of a Boar* has footnotes that echo distantly (to this ear) some of Joyce's alchemy. Take this example, in which Norfolk transforms the ordinary stuff of his research into prose poetry: A pre-Homeric hero in the text muses about the "early drop" of apples. A footnote below begins, "Summer, even late summer, is not autumn. An apple is not a quince. . . ." That the note continues on with a sober, scholarly justification of those introductory sentences does not diminish our pleasure in their initial, strange beauty. See Lawrence Norfolk, *In the Shape of a Boar* (London: Weidenfeld & Nicolson, 2000), p. 23, note 88. (The text of *In the Shape of a Boar,* incidentally, has a double

memorable than any of Ferber's dutiful sentences, and should take anti-footnoters like Sullivan down a rhetorical peg or two.

But lest *Finnegan's Wake* be dismissed as elitist stuff by the common folk at *The New Yorker,* and thus by association the footnote, let us ask our own rhetorical question: Have none of that crew taken time off from reading Ferber to dip into the detective novels of S. S. Van Dine?

Van Dine was the pseudonym of Willard Wright, who wasted the first half of his life writing poetry, philosophy, and art criticism; but he turned things around in the 1920s by making money out of a series of best-sellers featuring the brilliant man-about-town sleuth Philo Vance. Despite the sophistication of his fictional hero, Willard Wright was clearly intent on being no elitist James Joyce; "I Used to Be a Highbrow but Look at Me Now" was the title of an article he wrote for *American Magazine* in 1929.[60] No highbrow, he nonetheless often engaged in footnoting, and we are the beneficiaries of his "stooping" to them. Vance, baffled early on in *The Benson Murder Case,* smokes a cigarette and looks out at a "hazy June sky." For nearly a page he ruminates on the Shakespearean claim "murder will out," finally being reduced to Latin. A footnote quickly brings him down to earth: A former assistant commissioner of Metropolitan Police, London, has written in *The Saturday Evening Post:* "It is because murder will not out that the pleasant shock of surprise when it does out calls for a proverb to enshrine the phenomenon. The poi-

narrative: One story set in ancient Greece is followed by another set in the last months of the Second World War. Footnotes come frequently at first and then die out as we leave Greece—the accusatory implication being that we are more familiar with the Nazis of Germany than with the heroes of Greece.)

60. Available: http://www.britannica.com [26 February 2001].

soner who is brought to justice has almost invariably proved to have killed other victims without exciting suspicion. . . ."[61] What a comfort it is to know that this issue can be talked about without resort to a dead language.

The numerous examples of effective footnotes in novels and elsewhere do not seem to have slowed down the *New Yorker* gang;* they continued their harassment of annotators, as we will soon see when we turn our attention once more to the ongoing story of the poetic footnote.

---

61. S. S. Van Dine, *The Benson Murder Case: A Philo Vance Story* (New York: Charles Scribner's Sons, 1930), p. 112, note.

* We should note, however, the strange case of one of *The New Yorker*'s most esteemed writers, J. D. Salinger. *Franny and Zooey,* his interlocking stories, first appeared in the magazine; a few pages into "Zooey" a footnote, of all things, pushes its way into the narrative, in fact sprawling across the bottom of two pages. Salinger is suitably embarrassed; he begins, "The aesthetic evil of a footnote seems in order just here, I'm afraid." He then continues with information about the prior lives of the Glass children that the reader "may care to know. . . ." By no means do I want to suggest that the embarrassment explains *even in part* Salinger's subsequent years of seclusion in New Hampshire. J. D. Salinger, *Franny and Zooey* (Boston and Toronto: Little, Brown, 1961), pp. 52-3.

6

A Poetic Interlude II

THE NEED TO FOLLOW the main stream of footnotes running into and through the twentieth century has led us to ignore the eddies and backwaters of
modern poetry. Though no poetry, modern or traditional,
has made much of a splash in recent decades, the footnote
has been welcomed by some of the more innovative and
courageous poets, a fact that predictably has made anti-
avant-gardists nervous. As early as 1957 one of their leaders,
the novelist John Updike, warned that unsettling Haley's
comet would reappear in thirty years (he proved correct) and
that, in the meantime, we should beware of Marianne Moore
and John Berryman, both of whom had just published verse
to which notes were attached. In Updike's sky these were apparently also omens of disaster. Updike predicted: "the poem
of the future may well look like this."[1]

> Vernal Pride
> (A Sonnet)

The empty space below the title, Updike explains, is
"where the reader imagines the poem. After all, he ought to

---

1. John Updike, "Notes," *The New Yorker,* 26 January 1957, p. 28.

do *something.*[2] Then Updike supplies fourteen annotations of parodistic intent—precisely fourteen, a sonnet of notes.*

So unnerved is Updike that he is unable to peer back into the past any farther than he is able to discern the future. (Unlike Haley's comet, no blank sonnet with footnotes has appeared.) He finds in the past a single precedent for annotated poetry in "the desultory remarks T. S. Eliot affixed to the corpus of 'The Waste Land.'"[3] Updike then proceeds to make some desultory fun of one of the notes in particular: Eliot's explanation of the water-dripping song of the hermit thrush, *Turdus aonaldschkae pallasii,* is, according to Updike, "justly celebrated."[4] Had Updike pursued the matter, he would have found much earlier experimentation with poetic notes, and even a possible inspiration for those in "The Waste Land."

Updike would not have had to go back to our seventeenth-century pioneer of the footnote, Aphra Behn. A precedent can be found in the work of the Reverend George Crabbe, whose life extended into the nineteenth century, perhaps a century more understandable to someone like Updike, who has spent most of his time as a novelist. Despite his unfortunate name, Crabbe was a lyricist of some charm and a poet unafraid to

---

2. Ibid., p. 29.

* These footnotes are desultory entertainment rather like overheard cocktail talk. A lot of names are dropped but little real elucidation occurs. Hans Fehn, Baudelaire, John H. Trueman, and Branch Rickey and "a friend," Ruby Water, are mentioned without full identification, as if they are all equally well known. Would Gibbon have let Branch Rickey appear in a note without some sly reference to the artful Dodgers absconding to Los Angeles? Undoubtedly, we would have learned with gratitude his opinion of earthquakes and Bugs Bunny and much else. And think what Bayle would have extracted from Baudelaire's life. Would he have made do, as Updike does, with simply a quote?

3. John Updike, "Notes," *The New Yorker,* 26 January 1957, p. 28.

4. Ibid.

take the reader into his confidence. His verse is always thoroughly annotated, many of the notes anticipating Eliot's regard for nature. To take one example: After mentioning "sampirebanks" in his verse, Crabbe carefully notes, "The jointed glasswort, Saliconia, is here meant, not the true sampire, the *crithmum maritimum*."[5] Here one finds an honest workman at work: Unable to comfortably fit "jointed glasswort" into his meter, Crabbe admits it, and then uses annotation to meet the demands of art *and* science.

The notes of Crabbe's poetry have an interesting publishing history. Over a period of time, five volumes of his collected works appeared. In the first two Crabbe's notes are placed at the end of sections or "letters"; they are essentially endnotes. With the third volume, the notes find their way to the foot of each page. Apparently the demand for his annotations was strong enough to influence the publisher and even to affect Crabbe's usual good humor. Introducing one note he writes: "I am informed that some explanation is here necessary, though I am ignorant for what class of my readers it can be required."[6]

Crabbe's testiness did not stop the demand for notes. An edition a decade later appeared in which all of Crabbe's notes have been shifted to the bottom of the page, where they are joined by an extravagant number of notes by friends and editors. Crabbe's footnotes prove convenient but also to be useful dramatic devices that enhance the poetic text. Take, for example, a tale of love with the evocative title "Procrastination." A "prudent" woman, Dinah, promises her love to Rupert, a homespun man of good heart but little means.

---

5. George Crabbe, *The Works of The Rev. George Crabbe,* vol. II (London: John Murray, 1823), note 2, p. 17.

6. Ibid., note 1, p. 89.

Over time she finds that her desire for romance is replaced by her desire for the finer things in life she enjoys while living with a well-to-do aunt:

> . . . these comforts cherish'd day by day,
> To Dinah's bosom made a gradual way;
>   Till love of treasure had as large a part,
> As love of Rupert, in the virgin's heart.[7]

Crabbe interjects ". . . av'rice, like the poison-tree, / Kills all beside it, and alone will be. . . ." (And indeed, by the end of "Procrastination" Dinah is alone and forlorn.) A footnote immediately makes avarice not only deadly but also foreign, definitely not homespun. "Allusion is here made," the note tells us, "not to the well-known species of *sumach,* called the poison oak, or *toxicodendron,* but to the *upas,* or poison-tree of Java. . . ."[8] The close proximity to the text of this note is crucial; only the most determined reader would have wrenched himself away from the smooth and seductive tide of iambic pentameter to search out an *end*note. But with a *foot*note, even a reader who floats dreamily past the bobbing asterisk will be deposited eventually at the bottom of the page and be forced to confront the *unenglishness* of avarice.

Crabbe came from a background of little money and made himself into an apothecary and surgeon, an Anglican priest and chaplain, a student of botany and entomology, and a poet.[9] He was a serious, determined man, and so was his

---

7. George Crabbe, *The Works of The Rev. George Crabbe,* vol. III (London: John Murray, 1823), p. 76.

8. Ibid.

9. These details of Crabbe's life, and the ones that follow, have been lifted (as in *shoplifted,* perhaps) from a consistently amusing thumbnail sketch of him by Michael Schmidt. See Michael Schmidt, *Lives of the Poets* (New York: Alfred A. Knopf, 1999), pp. 340–5.

verse. Though appreciated by the eighteenth-century Doctor Johnson and the twentieth-century F. R. Leavis, Crabbe's verse produces a certain dutifulness in the responses of many conscientious readers.* One reader claims Crabbe makes Thomas Hardy seem cheerful.[10] William Hazlitt, a lighter-hearted contemporary of the poet, claimed Crabbe "rivets attention by being tedious."[11]

But his verse does rivet attention, and so too do his footnotes, perhaps particularly his footnotes. "A Lover's Journey" is a tale in rhymed couplets with the simplest of plots. A lover, John, sets out on horseback to see his "Laura." (Her given name is in fact Susan, but when he thinks of her he feels himself to be Petrarch; and she seeing him thinks of Shakespeare and calls him Orlando.) On the trip to see her, the landscape strikes Orlando as glorious; on the way back, having discovered she is "inconsistent" (as someone who has read Shakespeare is likely to be), this sudden, dear John finds the very same landscape to be gray and desolate. End of tale. "It is the soul that sees;" Crabbe writes, "the outward eyes / Present the object, but the mind descries. . . ."[12] A footnote to the poem performs this kind of mood change on the reader, thus making denial of Crabbe's metaphysical point impossible. The still happy Orlando comes across a patch of brown water stag-

---

* F. R. Leavis became notorious for asserting that there were four and *only* four great novelists in the English language prior to the twentieth century. Neither Laurence Sterne nor Charles Dickens make the list, though one of Dickens's novels is included in the canon. *If only Dickens had been more serious* seems to have been Leavis's sigh. For such a critic to take notice of Crabbe is high praise.

10. Michael Schmidt, *Lives of the Poets* (New York: Alfred A. Knopf, 1999), p. 340.

11. Quoted in ibid.

12. George Crabbe, *The Works of The Rev. George Crabbe,* vol. III (London: John Murray, 1823), p. 197.

nating in slimy mud. "Flora scarcely deigns to bloom. . . ."[13] but
Orlando nonetheless exclaims: "Various as beauteous, Nature,
is thy face . . . all that grows has grace. . . ."[14] A riveting footnote
intervenes. "The ditches of a fen so near the ocean are lined
with irregular patches of a coarse and stained lava; a muddy
sediment rests on the horse-tail and other perennial herbs,
which in part conceal the shallowness of the stream . . ." Had
the footnote stopped here, it would simply have been an interruption; but it continues: ". . . a fat-leaved pale-flowering
scurby-grass appears early in the year, and the razor-edged bull-
rush in the summer and autumn." Attention to details! "The
fen itself has a dark and saline herbage; there are rushes and *ar-
row-head*, and in a few patches the flakes of the cotton grass are
seen, but more commonly the *sea aster*, the dullest of that numerous and hardy genus . . ." A lesser artist would have been
content to settle for the easy irony of dull sea aster becoming
part of Orlando's beauteous Nature. Crabbe doesn't: ". . . a
thrift blue in flower, but withering and remaining withered till
the winter scatters it; the saltwort, both simple and shrubby; a
few kinds of grass changed by their soil and atmosphere, and
low plants of two or three denominations undistinguished in a
general view of the scenery . . ." By now only the least attentive
readers will fail to see that the footnote has wrenched us deliberately away from the poem with its echoes of the pastoral tradition and has placed us firmly in the grasp of the attentive
botanist. Science is not art, Crabbe argues; the scientist is not
the lover. Our mood has changed as dramatically as that of
Orlando when he returns as the chastened John from the feck-
less Susan. With understandable pride, though perhaps unnecessary thoroughness, Crabbe drives his point home: "and in

13. Ibid., p. 201.
14. Ibid., p. 202.

this case there arise from it effluvia strong and peculiar, half-saline, half-putrid, which would be considered by most people as offensive, and by some as dangerous; but there are others to whom singularity of taste or association of ideas has rendered it agreeable and pleasant."[15] "[T]he adept in Dutch interiors, hovels, and pig-styes must find in Mr. Crabbe a man after his own heart,"[16] Dr. Johnson has said. That his remark is praise is made plausible by the "Lover's Journey" tour-de-force, tell-it-like-it-is footnote.*

15. Ibid., p. 201.

16. Quoted in Michael Schmidt, *Lives of the Poets* (New York: Alfred A. Knopf, 1999), p. 340.

* A traditional use of the footnote has been as a depository of invidious comparisons. That encourages me here. Thomas Gray, the poet of the "country churchyard," died in 1771 when George Crabbe was seventeen and as yet unpublished. Gray shared with Crabbe a deep seriousness and some of the same sympathy for those who—as he put it—"kept the noiseless tenor of their way." He also employed footnotes at times and thus might be considered by some Crabbe's predecessor. Nothing could be farther from the case. Crabbe's notes, as we have seen, are part of the drama of the poem; Gray's simply supply information of the sort one might find on a playbill. They are for the most part, in fact, a species of name-dropping. (Those who believe name-dropping to be the coin of the literary world might hold that Gray's footnotes are a kind of specie.) The verse mentions a "grave Lord-Keeper" and a note tells us this is "Hatton, prefe'd by Queen Elizabeth for his graceful Person and fine Dancing. . . ." A certain Styack is named in the verse and a note gives him standing as "The House-Keeper. . . ." A character stands "as mute as 'poor Macleane,'" and we are dropped down to the bottom of the page to hear that Macleane is a famous "Highwayman hang'd the week before." (In this case it *is* notable that Gray, a facetious poet, keeps his iambic pentameter going by an elision of *hanged*.) The notes come in a rather short poem titled "A Long Story." (See Edmund Gosse, ed., *The Works of Thomas Gray* (New York: A. C. Armstrong & Son, 1885), pp. 83, 88, 89, respectively.) On a single page of "The Installation Ode," a "sad Chatillon" becomes (down below) "Mary de Valentia, Countess of Pembroke, daughter of Guy de Chatillon, Comte

George Crabbe's heroic and dogged example did not establish the poetic usefulness of the footnote; quite to the contrary, most poets in the centuries that followed avoided them.
Even the modern Updike's trio of fall guys, T. S. Eliot, John
Berryman, and Marianne Moore, lack the courage of their
convictions; their notes are never at the bottom of the page
but always, and almost apologetically, at the end of the poem
or the back of the book. Marianne Moore's timidity is the
most puzzling. She was as famous for the boldness of her
hats* as for the self-assurance of her verse. She had enough
confidence in herself to suggest automobile names to the
Ford Motor Company, and to receive a handsome emolument
for her work.† Yet her notes do not receive the prominent
placement that they clearly deserve. "A Note on the Notes"

---

de St. Paul in France; of whom tradition says that her husband, Audemar
De Valentia, Earl of Pembroke, was slain at a tournament on the day of
nuptials. She was the foundress of Pembroke College or Hall, under the
name of Aula Mariae de Valentia." On the next line we are hurried below
to hear that "Elizabeth de Burg, Countess of Clare, . . . wife of John de
Burg, son and heir of the Earl of Ulster, and daughter of Gilbert de Clare,
Earl of Gloucester, by Joan of Acres. . . ." And so on for some dozen words
and a couple of kings more. Back up in the verse we get to view a single
comma and an "And Anjou's" before being sent below again to learn that
Anjou is "Margaret of Anjou, wife of Henry the Sixth, foundress of
Queen's College." A line and a half later . . . but the point is made. (See
ibid., p. 95.) Had John Updike's acidic remarks on notes been directed at
this kind of performance, we all would applaud. Footnotes in works of literature must serve some dramatic—not simply informational—purpose.
  * An enormous tricorne too large to pack was one of her favorites and
a favorite of her readers. It identified her as surely as the boldly complicated line breaks of her verse. The first sentence of one of her stories is,
"I was leaving Boston wearing two hats. . . ." See Michael Schmidt, *Lives
of the Poets* (New York: Alfred A. Knopf, 1999), p. 631.
  † That Ford did not adopt Moore's suggestions does not lessen our sense
of a poet unafraid. The company did not choose to name the new model the

shows that she, and not just her publisher, was ambivalent about them. "[S]ince in anything I have written, there have been lines in which the chief interest is borrowed . . . acknowledgments seem only honest." But she finds herself unable to resist the Updike types who (she writes): "suggest that quotation marks are disruptive of pleasant progress" while others say they "are a pedantry or evidence of an insufficiently realized task." Her answer is to temporize by hiding the notes where they will not offend the peculiar sensibilities of those "annoyed by provisos, detainments, and postscripts. . . ."[17] As if much of poetry, and much of life for that matter, didn't delight and instruct precisely with its provisos, detainments, and postscripts; getting to the end of a poem or a life expeditiously is just what we do not want to do.

John Updike himself cannot dismiss Moore's notes out of hand. With perhaps a bit of bourgeois unease, a sense of "waste not, want not," he employs a domestic analogy and in the process turns the flamboyant Moore into a simple housewife doing chores next door. "[T]he effect of her poetry is that of a spanking-clean, well-swept attic, and naturally, if the attic is to stay tidy, there must exist a storeroom, under the eaves, where she can jumble the bulkier objects: the Webster's New International Dictionary's definition of 'wen'tle-trap', with a pretty engraving; the abridged texts of two sports columns by Arthur Daley (New York Times [sic], March 3, 1952, and March 1, 1955); a drawing from the hand of Giulio Gomez, a Spanish school child age 6. . . ."[18]

Resilient Bullet, The Intelligent Whale, Pastelogram, or Utopian Turtletop (to mention just a few of the poet's suggestions) and instead named it after Edsel Ford. The Edsel's spectacular failure to sell is poetic justice.

17. Marianne Moore, *The Complete Poems of Marianne Moore* (New York: Macmillan, Viking Press, 1958), p. 262.

18. John Updike, "Notes," *The New Yorker*, 26 January 1957, p. 27.

But stop right there. Six-year-old Giulio Gomez's drawing[19] is a wonder. An efficiently drawn snail with eyes popping up above its tiny head, forthright and assertive as one of Moore's tricornes, brings a mule skidding to a halt. Yes, the anatomy of the mule is suspiciously close to a horse's, but the ears are a small miracle of startledness, and the jockey crouched atop the mule has the confident ignorance that always precedes a pratfall. Gomez knows just what he is doing; this is a piece of art, not something to be tossed into an attic storeroom and forgotten.[*]

Because the poem "Tom Fool at Jamaica" is presently laid out across two pages by its fulsome publishers, there is plenty of room for the drawing, if not for the two sports columns. There it would catch the eye of the reader first, and set a nicely ambitious tone for the subsequent reading, a tone that mingles a child's charm with a child's glee in the occurrence of any adult comeuppance: a Thurber moment. "Be infallible at your peril, as the poem says, 'for your system will fail. . . .'"[20] A good motto for jockeys, poets, and a novelist-turned-critic.

It is not as if John Updike does not know better. He himself has frequently used footnotes in his novels and short stories, though perhaps not always to great effect. In one example, a

---

19. See Marianne Moore, *The Complete Poems of Marianne Moore* (New York: Macmillan, Viking Press, 1958), p. 284.

* This is a sore point with this writer. At college I was fortunate to become close friends with a gifted sculptor. His works were made from bits and pieces of scrap iron that had acquired a complex and arresting patina from days and nights spent outside weathering in the Vermont winters. A six-foot, sharp-edged figure particularly attracted me. My friend offered it to me with the proviso that I "keep it on view, don't just stick it in some attic." After several U-Haul moves and several awkward living arrangements the artwork ended up in my parents' dark attic; I have had a guilty conscience ever since. If only those who toss out Gomez's work would have had similar experiences.

20. See Marianne Moore, *The Complete Poems of Marianne Moore* (New York: Macmillan, Viking Press, 1958), p. 162.

mention of a sea occasions the rather uninformative note: "The Caribbean—hence its idyllic aspect."[21] In "Roger's Version" the narrator has mastered "a few dead languages" in order "to parade sequential moments of the obdurately enigmatic early history of Christianity before classrooms of the hopeful, the deluded, and the docile. . . ."[22] His defensive, donnish, world-weary, adjective-buttressed irony may in Updike's eyes—excuse the two forlorn footnotes that come halfway into the story: a Latin quotation in the text, "Rursusne omnia necessaria . . . ,"[23] and so forth, receives an unnecessary translation at the bottom of the page. (Unnecessary for the Latin scholar, of course, but also for the general reader, who simply wants to get on with a sensual, morally fraught episode.) The same is true when, only twelve pages later, an English passage, "Who ever is ashamed of Me. . . ."[24] is taken to the bottom of the page and converted back into its Latin.

Character development can excuse many sins. In Updike's *In a Month of Sundays* there is at least a week of footnotes. Some are inconsequential; the narrator, another minister, but this one with an exuberance that wins our trust, presents himself as "dwelling in outer darkness . . ." though, he adds, "I might be caught by the flare of a match or by a shouting[*] star. . . ." The asterisk attached to "shouting" is a terse and reluctant, "O.K. *CF.* Wm. Blake."[25] The point, of course, is not

21. John Updike, *Museums and Women and Other Stories* (New York: Alfred A. Knopf, 1972), p. 159.

22. John Updike, *Roger's Version* (New York: Alfred A. Knopf, 1986), p. 3.

23. Ibid., p. 157.

24. Ibid., p. 169. Nor is the plot furthered by a later footnote of twelve lines of sprawling Latin in small print. A still later note simply confirms what is already abundantly clear: The narrator's mind is hospitable to bawdy thoughts in two languages. See ibid., pp. 175-6 and 190.

25. John Updike, *A Month of Sundays* (New York: Alfred A. Knopf, 1975), p. 15.

that we care that the narrator (or Updike, for that matter) has hijacked an adjective from the poet, but that the narrator (and Updike, perhaps) *thinks* we might care. Other notes correct slips of the typewriter: "dry thoughts" brings us this: "Meant to type 'throats,' was thinking 'thoughts,' a happy Freudian, let it stand. . . ."[26] In the same paragraph, nineteen lines later, "eriddence" brings us "Intentional this time: riddance applied to credence."[27] A note that the narrator could have avoided had he been more interested in clean copy than the murky unconscious. Later, "the parsonage yare*" brings us a regretful, "My first slip in a week of Sundays. My yard of yore?"[28]

For exploiting notes at the bottom of the page as a place for quibbling (and in a contemporary context), Updike should get credit, of course, even in the face of his hostile remarks against the footnote. Art does not require consistency, and may despise it. Updike's defenders undoubtedly will claim that it is his characters and not the author himself who send the head bobbing up and down the pages. Yes, but . . . Dostoyevsky chose spiritually tormented and morally conflicted characters because he himself was tormented and conflicted; Swann could scarcely have delighted in the madeleine had his creator disliked its taste; and does anyone seriously believe that Joseph Heller felt anything but fear and loathing when flying combat missions? No, Updike is drawn to characters who are drawn to footnotes; a fact that makes his screed against notes puzzling.*

---

26. Ibid., p. 5.
27. Ibid.
28. Ibid., p. 180. See also pp. 14, 117, 180, and 201.
* Updike's *Museums and Women and Other Stories* has a set of endnotes as eclectic, if not as fulsome, as any employed by Marianne Moore. To my knowledge, Updike has never explained why notes are appropriate for

Updike's own verse betrays a retrograde preference for rhyme, regular verse, and puns;* perhaps his judgment on poetic notes would have been different had he encountered them first in *The Saga of Cap'n John Smith* instead of in "The Waste Land." Christopher Ward's *Saga* is admittedly a parody, and a rather long one at that. Nevertheless, it hints of an even more exciting future for the footnote, for within it is one of the few existent rhymed footnotes. In the text Cap'n Smith appears naked on the poop deck of his ship.

> He takes the center of the stage.
> And holds it with a haughty glance.
> Beside him it must be confessed,
> His rival seems much over dressed.

At the bottom of the page, Christopher Ward comments in a note:

> Good breeding is most manifest
> In people slightly underdressed.
> Indeed, did parvenus but know it
> That's quite the easiest way to show it.[29]

---

fiction and yet not for poetry if that is, in fact, his belief. His ambivalence toward religion and sex has been studied at great length; one can hope some attention soon might be given to his apparent ambivalence toward footnotes.

* This writer is not unaware of the aggressive group of poets who call themselves (sometimes) the New Formalists and who express a preference for traditional rhythm and even rhyme. In England such poets make up the mainstream of poetry; from their point of view, free verse and T. S. Eliot may appear retrograde. I won't argue except to say that to insist, as I think Updike's practices indicate he does, that rhyme and rhythm must be accompanied by punning traces back to the seventeenth century and thus *is* retrograde.

29. Christopher Ward, *The Saga of Cap'n John Smith: Being an account of His Service in the Warre in Hungaria with the Turks; his Single Combats with*

That more serious poets have not adopted the rhymed footnote probably has little to do with the skittishness of the tradition-bound artists such as Updike; however, if the current climate of opinion against the footnote is sustained, such experimentation is unlikely ever to be fully exploited. Poets have enough trouble finding publishers as it is; one could hardly blame them for refusing to challenge another of the publisher's shibboleths.

A parody, however, should not provide us with the last word on the poetic footnote; and, fortunately, we have the example of the prolific and complex and serious David Jones, son of a Welshman, casualty of World War I, and convert to Catholicism. Not one to take a lighthearted view of things, Jones's poetry is not to be taken lightly either. T. S. Eliot himself saw to the publishing of Jones's first major work, *In Parenthesis: seinnyessit e gledyf ym penn mameu;* for a later edition he supplied an introduction for the verse and placed a kind of High Anglican blessing on it. The notes for "In Parenthesis" at first may remind one of those of "The Waste Land" and, similarly, are confined to the back of the book. However much Eliot may have inspired Jones or given him license to annotate, Jones's notes soon impress by their greater number, their greater length, and their greater variety. The notes do become, as Eliot's do, a grab bag of odd, scholarly references; we pull out *Y Gododdin,* an early Welsh epical poem, Coleridge, Gerard Manley Hopkins, Milton's "Hymn on the Morning of Christ's Nativity," the title page of *Seinnyessit e gledyf,* Tolstoy, also the English carol "Green Grow the Rushes-o," the

---

three Turkish Champions, wherein he was victorious, and how he was taken Prisoner by the Turks and Sold for a Slave and of his Escape therefrom. Also his Expedition into Virginia and his Adventures there among the Savages; being in Peril of his life, but saved by an Indian Princess. Furthermore his Observations in New England (New York: Harper & Brothers, 1928), p. 24.

German carol *"Es ist ein Ros' entsprungen,"* the American music-hall song "Casey Jones," and, with perhaps a bow to T. S. Eliot, *The Golden Bough*. It is difficult to imagine, however, Eliot devoting a page to a detailed map of a war zone or becoming as personal as to refer to his mother. "My mother always says in February," Jones writes, "as a proper check to undue optimism: 'As the light lengthens / So the cold strengthens.'"[30]

It was not until 1974 in his last book, *The Sleeping Lord and Other Fragments,* that Jones was either willing or able to channel his annotational imagination into footnotes. An experiment that mixes what I take to be prose poetry with free verse, "The Tribune's Visitation," provides one example that I hope clinches my argument that the footnote is a dramatic device worthy of any contemporary poet's consideration. War fills Jones with both pity and contempt; in this verse he wanders between Roman and more recent times: ". . . but must I do a corporal's nagging, must I be scold, like a second cook . . . Are there no lance-jacks to demonstrate standing orders?" is a prose poetry introduction to the following verse:

Does the legate need to do
what he delegates?
Must those with curial charge
be ever prying on a swarm of vicars
or nothing goes forward?
Must tribunes bring gunfire to centurions or else there's no
Parade?[31]

---

30. See David Jones, *In Parenthesis: seinnyessit e gledf ym penn mameu* (New York: Chilmark Press, 1961), p. 191, note 4; p. 195, note 15; p. 193, note 5; p. 191, note 1; p. 196, note 2; p. 203, note 11; p. 205, note 17 (for two of the references); p. 204, note 15; p. 192; and p. 194, note 12.

31. David Jones, *The Sleeping Lord and Other Fragments* (London: Faber & Faber, 1974), p. 48.

The poet is full of questions but so too is the reader. Jones has made us uneasy. In what era is the voice (or voices) placed, and is it anger, pity, or pride the voice(s) express? We are up in the air. A footnote at "gunfire" brings us down (literally) to earth: "This term that survived from the Regular Army and was familiar enough to soldiers of the new armies throughout the 1914–18 War, may by now be obsolete." The First World War has soldiers of *new* armies! Jones, with a fist thumping on the page, is telling us war and its horror are always present tense, never past tense, never past. *Gunfire* may be obsolete. The word and the reality are deliberately merged here; the word is not obsolete nor will it be obsolete until the reality is obsolete. Jones's blunt irony hits us—as the footnote intended it to—like a blunt instrument. Jones uses footnotes to multiply points of view and to gain emotional leverage. Poets are currently in doubt as how to proceed in a world in which there seems no place to stand, no lever long enough to move it; they would do worse than to go back to the brave poetry and brave annotations of David Jones.*

---

* A fine and adventuresome prose poet, a friend of mine, recently brought my attention to the work of Gad Hollander, whose annotation and prose poems deserve close analysis—which, unfortunately, they will not receive here. See Gad Hollander, "From /ʔe buk uv kraiz/" (*untitled: a magazine of prose poetry*, www.poetrypress.com, 2000), pp. 11–25. It may be that prose poets are particularly attracted to annotation, though my prose poet friend is adamantly against their use; the reason for his opposition is the stale one that anything important can and should be in the text proper. (That argument would apply to parentheses as well; anything important can and should be said unparenthetically. I have not consulted my friend about parentheses, however.) This particular prose poet is a publisher as well as a poet, which may explain his antagonism to the footnote.

7

Toward the Virtual Footnote

FOR DEVOTEES OF THE FOOTNOTE the new millennium deserved the fireworks and cork-popping of its start. The year 2000, despite its zeros, was not for nothing. A footnote made the front page of a major American newspaper. BUSH WINS ELECTION[*] was the *Boston Globe* banner headline for Monday, November 27, 2000. The asterisk led the eye to the subheadline [*]PENDING GORE CHALLENGES, POSSIBLE SUPREME COURT RULING.[1] A more thorough search of newspaper files than this writer has conducted might reveal an earlier headline asterisk, but this is for now a footnote first.

The parent company of the *Globe, The New York Times,* has carried on into the new millennium its habit of occasionally employing "footnotes" in the "Style" section of its Sunday magazine. Thus, the day before the *Globe* breakthrough, one could find in a "Style" caption nestled between two photos: "Linda McCartney [1,2] self-portrait and her picture of Mary,

---

1. *The Boston Globe,* Monday, 27 November 2000, p. 1. Some readers may question whether a note at the bottom of a headline instead of at the bottom of the page constitutes a proper footnote; however, this writer believes a certain latitude should be given the trailblazing editors at the *Globe.*

when she was a toddler."[2] The [1,2] references have to be tracked down across nine pages of ads and text until they show up later under the title "Footnotes" *(sic)*. But the search rewards the dogged reader with notes of substance. [1] mutates into [1a] in the short time it takes to flip the pages; it allows us to view a picture of the grown-up Mary, and to learn she carries on her mother's camera-toting tradition. Mary, we are told, has an upcoming assignment to shoot a portrait series for the mag *Marie Claire*. A further mutation takes place (because of absentminded proofing, we assume) and so we next have [1] becoming [7(b)]. An "updated Leica R8" is shown "available at B&H photo, 420 Ninth Avenue ($1,895, body only)."[3] No price is offered for those who might want the Leica's lens and moving parts as well as its body.

So determined to encourage annotation are the *Times* editors that they also have been putting out special magazine editions that contain dozens of "footnotes." The contents page of their "Spring HomeDesign *[sic]*," for example, lists much that might be expected: "They Did Windows," "Candyland," "Ode a la Mode," and so forth. Suddenly, in the midst of all of that, there it is: "Footnotes" with a byline, no less: Pilar Viladas. Two titles later is: "Footnotes" by Stephen Mihm.[4] Flip past an ad featuring a spacious black-and-white kitchen to where the contents page continues and you find "Footnotes" by Marjorie Rosen.[5]

---

2. *The New York Times Magazine,* Sunday, 26 November 2000, p. 131. See also the "footnotes" in "Men's Fashions of the Times," *The New York Times Magazine,* Part 2, fall 2000.

3. *The New York Times Magazine,* Sunday, 26 November 2000, p. 140.

4. *The New York Times Magazine,* Part 2, spring 2000, p. 16.

5. Ibid., p. 20. For the record, Ms. Viladas is also listed as editor of the magazine; I am curious as to whether she originated the *Times* footnote page, and how much (if any) encouragement she received.

Three writers have been given a chance to try their hand at annotating! Turn to page 78 and Ms. Viladas's note tells us (among other things) that the photographers of the story were given "a breakfast on the terrace, with fresh guava juice." Keep going to page 100 and Ms. Rosen tells us that Eleanor Lambert, "the doyenne of fashion publicists," drinks for breakfast hot water and lemon juice from "a glass with two dice in its fake bottom . . . and orange juice in a larger Venetian glass." Back on page 92 Mr. Mihm's notes, featuring lamps ranging in price from $300 to $1,350,[6] are tasteful, though they fail to mention breakfast.

Admittedly, these notes refer to little squibs of photographs within the "footnote" page instead of going back directly to original story, but these "footnotes" as well as the previous notes clearly are *The Times'* way of preparing public opinion for more extensive and genuine footnotes.[*] When Martin Amis's heavily footnoted memoir, *Experience: A*

---

6. Ibid., in order of appearance above, pp. 78, 100, 92. No art form is without its awkward moments, and this is one for the footnote. The page numbers all appear in the paragraph above; nevertheless, some readers intending to check sources may expect to find the numbers in a citation. This writer prefers to risk the slight annoyance of redundancy rather than take the larger risk of inadequate annotation.

The New York Times has been indefatigable. Anthony Grafton's trail-blazing work, *The Footnote: A Curious History,* was given not one but two deservedly laudatory reviews. (See Christopher Lehmann-Haupt, *The New York Times,* Thursday, 27 November 1997, p. E16, and David McKitterick, Sunday, 7 December 1997, section VIII, p. 86.) But years before that *The Times* fired a shot across the bow of the anti-footnote dreadnought by publishing a fervent pro-footnote op-ed piece of mine. (See *The New York Times,* Sunday, 23 August 1981.) Lest anyone think this has lent a bias to my view of the newspaper, let me say that the two reviews of *The Footnote* shared a serious failing: Neither one of them picked up on the unconscious hostility toward the footnote exhibited by Anthony Grafton (see chapter 1, "The Endangered Footnote").

Memoir, recently appeared, *The Times* greeted it with an enthusiastic review on the front page of its "The Arts" section.
The reviewer begins by lauding Amis for his "dazzling,
chameleonesque command of language" and "his willingness to
tackle large issues" and for "his unforgiving, heat-seeking eye";
but by the third sentence she has a chance to applaud the book

---

More recently *The Times* footnote campaign has remained enthusiastic
but has become rather clumsy, perhaps. A prominent, front-page story
recounts sympathetically the bold attempt of some American lawyers
and judges to remove citations from within legal texts and affix them to
the bottom of the pages. Such sensible depositions of notes should be
applauded; unfortunately, the whole affair associates in the public mind
the footnote with a profession held by the general public in quite low es-
teem. The *O.E.D.* informs us that *lawyer* refers—in an English dialect—to
"a long bramble" and in New Zealand to "certain creeping plants."
Enemies of the footnote are masters of guilt by association; they easily
would stoop to making an association by way of lawyers between the
footnote and scratchy, creepy low life. (See William Glaberson, *The New
York Times,* Sunday, 8 July 2001, p.1).
  The reader might also want to take a look at Jennifer Dunning, "Dance
Review: An Incomprehensible Work? How About Some Footnotes?" *The
New York Times,* Monday, 15 January 2001, p. B10. The review says
Gabriele Kroos's dance program in Soho "tackled large themes, complete with the dance equivalent of footnotes." Dance, of course, cannot
present footnotes in any literal sense without appearing simply silly;
that Dunning finds the footnote analogy compelling, however, suggests
that "annotation" is a very useful metaphor in these days of Postmodern
thought and art. One of the dances, Dunning claims, ". . . proved that
the incomprehensible can be made enticing"; no better summary statement of the Postmodern program can be made. The apotheosis of the
footnote took place on April 17, 2001. On that date a clue to *The New
York Times* Crossword Puzzle was "Where a star might lead?" The answer
to this poetic hint will come as no surprise to the reader—a footnote.
Notice also should be taken of *The Times'* urban neighbor, *The Nation.*
This outspoken magazine is not given to either qualifying or footnoting
its arguments. The contested presidential election, though, so stimulated it that at least one of its articles sputtered into notes. See Vincent
Bugliosi, "None Dare Call It Treason," *The Nation,* 5 February 2001. A
cursory search through recent copies of the right-wing counterpart to

as an "entertainingly footnoted volume,"[7] a placement in the hierarchy of praise that must hearten all literary annotators.

And in fact *Experience* is just the book with which to start off the new millennium; its notes are as numerous as they are artful and dramatic. A simple example: Amis, well into the book, takes a look at the correspondence that passed between his aging father and the poet Philip Larkin and assesses their relationship. Kingsley Amis, novelist, and Larkin, poet, had a long, complicated, and competitive friendship. "But what stays with you is the sense that the two of them . . . are at last transparent to each other. They are finally equal, equal before God and a godless death, and also physically and—for the first time—sexually equal."[8] An asterisk takes us to a note that begins: "In all likelihood this question deserves more attention than the longish footnote I am going to give it."[9] The "longish" note continues for another 323 words, not one of which is wasted. We learn of Nabokov's division of all people between those who sleep well, "complacent dopes," and those who are "great twisting insomniacs (like himself). . . ."[10] We hear a character in one of the many novels of Martin Amis's father divide humanity into the attractive and the unattractive; and we are presented with a Larkin unpublished poem that rings changes on the theme of "good-looking girls"; and then, and only then, we come to

The Nation, The National Review, has failed to turn up any similar sputters; it is to be hoped that the liberal reputations of *The Times* and the *Globe,* and the cantankerous reputation of *The Nation,* do not convince conservatives that the footnote's defense is solely a left-wing cause.

7. Michiko Kakutani, "Books of the Times: For Writers, Father and Son, Out of Conflict Grew Love," *The New York Times,* Tuesday, 23 May 2000, p. B1.

8. Martin Amis, *Experience* (New York: Hyperion, 2000), p. 245.

9. Ibid., note.

10. Ibid.

Kingsley Amis's wintry remark: "I am getting ugly now because I am getting old."[11]

But Martin Amis is not done yet; his annotating art is sly. On the next page he quotes a letter of his; the name Sally[12] appears in it unadorned except for an asterisk. Below we find simply: "My sister,"[13] the shortest note of the book, and perhaps an unnecessary one—the information could have been supplied within the text, certainly. But a neat comic effect results in the short note coming after the long and winding road of the previous one, and after a long note that complains it may be in fact too short. In the silent movies a baggy-pants man or a beautifully polished grand piano may bump down a long, twisting staircase and come banging to a stop at the bottom step. A pause. Dead quiet. The pause stretches out. Then the man or piano bumps to the floor with one last, tired bang.

Amis is a self-conscious practitioner of his craft. He worries that life is "amorphous" and he admits to a "novelist's addiction to seeing parallels and making connections." That and "an inner urgency," he hopes, will allow *Experience* to "give a clear view of the geography of a writer's mind."[14] Raw experience pulled into the mind is to be given shape; and what is revealed is the shape of the mind in the way molten ore reveals the mold into which it is poured. But Amis is not foolish enough to let it rest at that; he alludes parenthetically to his need also for footnotes "to preserve the collateral thought."[15] Bayle and a thousand other earlier annotators

11. Ibid., p. 246, continuation of note.

12. Ibid., p. 246.

13. Ibid., note, marked by an asterisk and directly below the continuation of the previous page's note; it is easy to overlook, which may be intended by Martin Amis as part of the joke.

14. Ibid., p. 7.

15. Ibid.

should be imagined in the heavens above singing hosannas when they hear those words: collateral thought, exactly.

The mind may give shape to experience but it is not a mold, it is not neat, it never settles down; it disorganizes as it organizes; and, having blazed one trail, it instantly takes off in another direction. Its mother's milk is mixed metaphors, oxymorons, red herrings, the bumping into hornets' nests, and the stepping on toes. Footnotes can represent that trait of mind; in that sense footnotes represent organized confusion.*

To appreciate fully the art of Martin Amis's annotation, we must force ourselves to look squarely at a sad and fearsome event in Amis's life. A cousin of Martin's, Lucy Partington, to whom he was very close and who was a remarkable woman by all accounts, disappeared when she was a young woman. For some twenty years her fate was unknown; then police discovered she had been grotesquely murdered by a serial killer, ". . . one of the most prolific . . . in British history. . . ."[16] Amis was deeply affected by the disappearance and the murder, and now is compelled to write about it. But how? How do you bring attention to the cousin you loved and the fearful facts of her death without ceding to the killer a tabloid prominence that overshadows the cousin and the grief? (Don't most news accounts of murder end up paying more attention to the grisly details of the murder scene than to the life of the victim and even more attention to the murderer than to the victim?)

Amis's moral and artistic dilemmas are solved by foot-

---

* *Collateral*, of course, has several meanings. This reader assumes Amis's use is synonymous with "accompanying," "auxiliary," "additional," "secondary," and synonymous with each of those, not just one of them. It seems unlikely he could mean "collateral" in any narrower sense; that would make him a much less sophisticated annotator than is plausible given the other literary skills he demonstrates.

16. Martin Amis, *Experience* (New York: Hyperion, 2000), p. 62.

notes. Lucy Partington's disappearance is brought up early in the book; the killer's name, Frederick West, is briefly mentioned. From then on, as Lucy reappears in the text in many situations and under many lights, poignant and witty, counselor and tease, her killer for the next 120 pages or so is mentioned only in footnotes and only as a killer. And then, and only then, a chapter opens with: "1995 did not stand on ceremony. It announced itself, on the first of January, with the prison suicide of Frederick West. (And in death, as it were, he drifts up from the footnotes and into the text.) . . ."[17] (The ellipsis is Amis's as his voice trails off.) From then on the killer again is allowed a place only in footnotes.

The clear usefulness of footnotes that Amis has demonstrated has stimulated reviewers other than those in *The New York Times* to make special notice of them. In the *London Review of Books* John Lanchester, a novelist himself, mentions ". . . the antic parade of footnotes. . . ." found in *Experience*.[18] And sure enough, Lanchester employs his own asterisk; his note below begins, perhaps a trifle optimistically: "There are a lot of footnotes about at the moment, and I thought I'd hop onto the bandwagon before it gathered any more speed."[19] And sure enough again: The footnote's subsequent mention of Dave Eggers's memoir, *A Heartbreaking Work of Staggering Genius,* brings us a second asterisk and a simple note below the first one: "To be reviewed in a forthcoming issue of LRB."[20] No footnote devotee would want to shove anyone off any bandwagon, but Lanchester's enthusiasm should be greeted with some skepticism.

---

17. Ibid., p. 195.

18. John Lanchester, "Be Interesting!" *London Review of Books,* 6 July 2000, p. 6.

19. Ibid., note.

20. Ibid., note to first note. Of course, it might be the *LRB* editors' doing; they may have seized the chance for a free plug for an upcoming is-

The "antic" possibilities of footnotes have blinded John Lanchester to their wide-ranging, serious, dramatic capabilities. "The footnotes in Amis's book," he writes, "are often short diversions into memory or literary criticism away from the main emotional axis."[21] No, this is to entirely miss the painful story of Lucy Partington and the importance of footnotes to its proper telling. Lanchester continues in his note with a mini review of *A Heartbreaking Work of Staggering Genius* in which—he claims—footnotes are used "to deflect, or escape from, the strength of [the narrator's] own feelings; which isn't a zillion miles away from Amis's use of them."[22] The hyperbole of "zillion" suggests an unease on Lanchester's part, a need to shout when a quiet statement would do; and his unease is justified. Not only has he mischaracterized Amis's annotation, but he has overstated Eggers's use of them as well; a careful examination of *A Heartbreaking Work* has turned up only two footnotes, one of which is marginal at best.[*] Two footnotes! The "footnotes" of Lanchester's review barely earns its plural designation.

Lanchester includes footnotes among the "huge repertoire

---

sue. Money talks, and even *The New Yorker*, which normally keeps its page bottoms immaculate, may listen: An ad in a recent issue asserts: "Money management is what we do." And a large, easily visible, red asterisk floats above the period; it leads the reader to the next page and below a photo of a white-haired Odysseus type hugging a surfboard. The note says: "Technically speaking, we can also make dreams come true." See *The New Yorker*, 12 February 2001, pp. 14, 15.

21. Ibid., first note.

22. Ibid., note.

* The one unquestionable Eggers footnote is part of what amounts to a book promotion. The text offers to send five dollars to the first two hundred readers of *A Heartbreaking Work* on receiving a proof of purchase. The note then declares the obvious and rubs it in: "It should go without saying that if you've checked this book out from the library, or are reading it in paperback, you are much, much too late." See Dave Eggers, *A Heartbreaking Work of Staggering Genius* (New York, London, Sydney, and

of Post-Modern tricks"[23] used by Eggers; and certainly the Postmodern sensibility delights in double narrative, second thoughts, multivoice effects, palimpsests, distancing devices, disjunction, irony, and the jokey, all of which the footnote certainly facilitates. This tendency of the Postmodern to do the double take becomes "hyper" when it hooks up to computers with their frightening power to redo and undo, pop in, pop out, and pop up, and digress and wander. As the footnote reconfigures itself for the digital world, opportunity and danger are waiting side by side for it.

FORGET FOOTNOTES. HYPERLINK.[24] is the headline of the ever-alert *New York Times;* a subheading adds: OLD MEDIA, MEET NEW MEDIA. The alarming headline is somewhat misleading, though the reader is quite accurately informed that some publishers had been scrubbing their books clean of "messy" footnotes. "Annotation was out; breezy uninterrupted prose was in."[25] The reader has also been accurately informed that, after this cleansing had gone on for some time, a Tim Berners-Lee created the World Wide Web. And because of that strange invention, Ms. Bader thinks she can say: "Soon the missing footnotes would have a home." Now that the "old media" has met the "new media," the footnote, when evicted from the book by publishers and lazy scholars, is not to be out in the street. No, it is to move into a nice tract house on

---

Singapore: Simon & Schuster, 2000), p. xxv. Even now, in this time of escalating commercialization, a time when Madison Avenue types eye lustfully any blank space on television or magazines or the Internet or popcorn bags or public buses or U.S. Mail boxes or T-shirts, pants, and computer floppy disks or . . . and so on and so forth; even now the thought that the footnote might become a billboard strikes this consumer as absurd. And yet see also above, note 20, page 142.

23. Ibid.

24. Jenny Lyn Bader, "Forget Footnotes. Hyperlink." *The New York Times,* Sunday, 16 July 2000, Section 4 (Week in Review), p. 1.

25. Ibid.

the Web; it is to spend the new millennium sitting in an arm-
chair in front of a warm fireplace, children's voices drifting
down from upstairs, and reading a newspaper—*The New York
Times,* presumably. The years ahead for the footnote are going
to be the 1950s—but wired.

A couple of paragraphs later the confusion is compounded
and, at the same time, explained. "Indeed the Web has not
only revived the footnote, it has spawned a cross-referencing
craze that renders the formerly complete media event into a
reference-laden, link-dependent, list-spewing, wallflower
waiting to be courted by the next available annotator."[26] The
actual footnote,* the numbered or asterisked citation or bit
of commentary, can be used on the Web, and can be called
"footnote" without fostering confusion even if it is accompanied by bright colors, illustrations, and the constant click-
ing of mice.

On the other hand, the art of annotation is stretched into
shapelessness when made analogous to the exuberant cross-
referencing, list making, and site linking that occur on a Web
crisscrossed with blinking, neonlike come-ons for insurance
companies and astrologers and auctions and weather reports
and everything else under the digital sun.

The footnote either becomes so new an entity on the Web
that it ceases to be a footnote or stays so much the same old

---

26. Ibid.

* The thing that just now tilted your head downward or got you to adjust
the book page upward. Ms. Bader herself mixes to good effect the book
footnote and the hypertext reference in her article. For example: "Small
children who would normally not read books with footnotes until secondary school know their way around bright blue hyperlinks." *Hyperlinks* is indeed printed in a pleasantly bright blue and underlined in blue in the
hypertext manner. The finger itches to click-click a mouse. Instead a reference mark beside the blue leads to the bottom of the article and a pleasant
if conventional note: "Hyperlinks may lead to lovely places unless the links
themselves have expired. Then they lead to error messages."

footnote that it is likely to be overlooked amid the digital glit-
ter. One can find on-line, for example, Joseph Conrad's *Heart
of Darkness*—and the novel has a particularly appropriate title
for our first venture into cyberspace. This version of the novel
is intended for high school students or college freshmen,
some of whom may be part of Ms. Bader's generation of children who happily make their way deep into hyperlinks.

They will find this stopover at *Heart of Darkness* a bit
tame, though it *is* useful, and it *is* tastefully done. The illustrations and the text glow with a peaceful and welcome
daisy yellow; the words in the text that occasion notes are
discreetly underlined; if the print of the text is a trifle small
for the easiest reading,* the "footnotes," reached with a
simple click, make fine reading. Click on the novel's first
mention of Kurtz, a central figure in the story, for instance,
and a bar at the bottom of the screen shows three paragraphs of careful description of Kurtz, the words set
against a restful blue background. The note is carefully labeled CHARACTERS to alert you to the fact that other characters in the story can be "accessed." You can also click to
THEMES IN HEART OF DARKNESS, which instantly appear
against a soothing green—and high school students and
college freshman can use soothing often, maybe even continually.[27] The footnotes act like nothing so much as a discreet butler bringing you a note on a silver tray.

But what if Bader's Web-experienced children go to www.ya-

---

* A teen's eyes, of course, might judge the type more favorably than
this writer's eyes.

27. Joseph Conrad (no date), *Heart of Darkness* [Originally published in
Blackwood Magazine in 1899, February, March, and April. Subsequently
published in 1902 in *Youth: A Narrative, and Two Other Stories.*] Available:
http://www.acsu.buffalo.edu/csicseri/ [10 February 2001]. For the most
part the annotation's format follows the suggestions of Xia Li and Nancy
B. Crane, *Electronic Styles: A Handbook for Citing Electronic Information*

hoo.com instead of www.acsu.buffalo.edu/csicseri/? A big red
YAHOO! greets them. Intense blue lettering is everywhere: YA-
HOO MAIL. YAHOO! DOMAINS: CLAIM YOUR NAME. GET THE Y!
STOCK MARKET TOOLBAR. YAHOO! SHOPPING: FROM APPAREL TO
TOYS. Rhymes and exclamation marks are everywhere.

And so many times, at so many places, your cursor turns
unbidden into an eager hand with an exclamation point after
it—as if grasping a bright future for you. A news box has:
JERUSALEM CAR BOMB INJURES ONE. A Marketplace box has: BID
ON A CELEBRITY SMOOCH: ELTON JOHN. . . . Perhaps not such
an attractive smooch choice for our teenagers. Well then:
Britney? There is a list of people to smooch.

And that's without going to the serious stuff, the Arts and
Humanities section, the Society and Culture section . . . or go-
ing to the Fantasy games including Survivor and Extreme
Football . . . or going to local Yahoo!s in China or San
Francisco Bay . . . and so on and so forth.

The conventional footnote is in trouble. Going to acsu.buf-
falo.edu is going on a nature walk with your eighth-grade
class; yahoo.com is hanging out with your friends at the mall.

We know annotating is never going to win if it has to com-
pete with shopping. Moreover, we know footnotes like anything else on the Web can go *poof!* and disappear. Li and Crane
in *Electronic Styles: A Handbook for Citing Electronic Information*
give fair warning. Again and again the model citations they
supply end with "Available" and then the date the site was last
accessed. Web sites, like milk cartons, need expiration dates.

And like "the mall," the Web is educating our preteens,
tweens, and teenagers—and our college students. "The Effect of

---

(Medford, N.J.: Information Today, 1996). Nothing shows the growth and
seriousness of the hyperlink challenge to the footnote more clearly than a
comparison of this recent edition of *Electronic Styles* with an earlier one. A
1993 edition ran to 65 pages; the 1996 edition needed 213 pages.

the Web on the Undergraduate Citation Behavior 1996–1999," a thoughtful and alarming article, appeared on the Web some time before its publication in *The Journal of the American Society for Information Sciences* (JASIS). This writer and his readers have to be grateful for the Web: The article would not have been available in time for it to be quoted in this book if we had to wait for *JASIS* to arrive in the mail; moreover, the Web site has a color photo of the authors that shows them as youthful, friendly, and candid—and sets them looking perfectly at home in front of rows of computers. They are certainly not old fogies who have it in for the new, digital, bookless study hall. Such a photo and the information it conveys are not likely to make it into an academic journal. And it is useful to know they are still relatively young given the import of the article.

The two authors may look friendly but they do not pull any punches. Undergraduate papers in microeconomics between 1996 and 1998 show a serious deterioration in the students' citation behavior. Book citations have dropped dramatically; newspaper citations have increased. "Web citations checked in 2000 revealed that only 18% of URLs cited in 1996 led to the correct Internet document. For 1999 bibliographies, only 55% of URLs led to the correct document."[28] Students are becoming accustomed to Web "cites" and Web sites are going *poof!* left and right.

One site, purl.access.gov/gpo/lps2768, may have been designed to make the same point. It is supposed to be home for

---

28. Philip M. Davis and Suzanne Cohen, "The Effect of the Web on Undergraduate Citation Behavior 1996–1999," available: http://people.cornell.edu/pages/pmd8/ [14 February 2001]. The article should also be available in vol. 52, no. 4 (15 February 2001), of *The Journal of the American Association for Information Science.* This author wishes to thank Nancy Thompson for bringing this article to his attention as well as for her many other helpful e-mailed suggestions—and yes, this author, for all his worries about the Web, appreciates its convenience and speed.

a "Report of the Committee on Automatic and Technology's Subcommittee on Policy and Programs concerning standard electronic citations, 1997";* one would hope, of course, that the report would bring some reassurance that the problem of disappearing sites is being addressed. A search, though, brings forth: "The requested . . . has been deactivated and cannot be resolved." Well, neither can the worry of conscientious annotators be resolved.

Doubts of the permanency of virtual footnotes remain with this writer even though two experienced and inventive computer experts have offered reassurances. The first, John Blankenbaker, a longtime advocate of the computer who has been designated the creator of "the first commercially available personal computer" by The Computer Museum of Boston, speaks quite directly to the problem. "How permanent is the Web and the information that it has?" he asks. "I do not believe it is permanent," he answers without blinking an eye. Even if Web sites (or Web cites, perhaps) are backed up by disks of one kind or another, technological changes can make them unreadable in the future: "Who can read a five-and-a-half-inch floppy disk now?" Mr. Blankenbaker asks rhetorically and then adds: Paper and microfilm "aren't permanent either . . . the old vellum has stood the test of time better than anything . . . even . . . marble inscriptions are disappearing. . . ."[29] The implication, of course, is that literacy, literature, scholarship, the footnote itself have survived the crumbling of marble, acid rain on paper, and the whims of publishers: Footnotes will survive the Web. I am not reassured.

---

* The report, however, is supposed to be available on microfilm, which simply reinforces the remarks made below about the need for storage redundancy.

29. Personal communication (e-mail) to this writer, available only on nonvellum paper insecurely filed.

The second expert, John Laux, a digital technologist and theorist, offers a plan that I am going to call the Laux Redundancy Plan: Footnotes at one site could be also stored in, say, fifty other sites around the world. "So ten years down the line, if we lose twenty of them we can still retrieve your [footnotes],"[30] a kind of safety net will be hung under the threatened footnote.

We know we are going to want to preserve some footnotes for centuries; for these treasures, fifty backups seems a perilously small number. One hundred or even one thousand backup sites might be more sensible; we might indeed hope to keep a backup on microfilm or even vellum. Obviously what is called for at this historic juncture is a well-funded, broadly representative international committee to explore and establish a policy for the encouragement and preservation of the venerable (and vulnerable) footnote. A first step toward such a committee might be an informal Web site to facilitate networking and planning; this Footnotes On Redundancy site, or FOR, should be simple and accessible; its address—if not already taken—should be www.footnoteredundancy.com.

This site can begin the necessary organizing and people-to-people linking that a successful footnote movement will require. Success is not a certainty, but we can take hope from the long history of the footnote; the footnote is a tough old bird and is not going the way of the auk or the dodo; surely it is going to learn to fly once again in virtual reality—proud, virile, and redundant.

---

30. Personal communication (e-mail) to this writer.
Note: Readers desiring a bibliography to this work should look for my next book, *A History of Bibliographies.*